JUDGE
FOR YOURSELF

Catherine
the
Great

CHRISTINE HATT

WORLD ALMANAC® LIBRARY

Please visit our web site at: www.worldalmanaclibrary.com
For a free color catalog describing World Almanac® Library's list
of high-quality books and multimedia programs, call 1-800-848-2928 (USA)
or 1-800-387-3178 (Canada). World Almanac® Library's fax: (414) 332-3567.

Library of Congress Cataloging-in-Publication Data

Hatt, Christine.
    Catherine the Great / by Christine Hatt.
        p. cm. — (Judge for yourself)
    Summary: A biography of the German princess who became the absolute ruler of the Russian empire
and won for herself the reputation of being a great enlightened monarch.
    Includes index.
    ISBN 0-8368-5535-3 (lib. bdg.)
    1. Catherine II, Empress of Russia, 1729–1796—Juvenile literature. 2. Russia—History—Catherine II, 1762–1796—
Juvenile literature. 3. Empresses—Russia—Biography—Juvenile literature. [1. Catherine II, Empress of Russia,
1729-1796. 2. Kings, queens, rulers, etc. 3. Russia—History—Catherine II, 1762–1796. 4. Women–Biography.]
    I. Title. II. Series.
    DK170.H375   2003
    947'.063'092—dc21   2003045006

This North American edition first published in 2004 by
World Almanac® Library
330 West Olive Street, Suite 100
Milwaukee, WI 53212 USA

This U.S. edition copyright © 2004 by World Almanac® Library. Original edition published in Great Britain by
Evans Brothers Limited. Copyright © 2002 by Evans Brothers Limited, 2A Portman Mansions, Chiltern Street,
London W1U 6NR, United Kingdom. This U.S. edition published under license from Evans Brothers Limited.

Consultant: Janet M. Hartley
Editors: Nicola Barber and Jinny Johnson
Design: Mark Holt
Maps: Tim Smith
Production: Jenny Mulvanny
Picture research: Julia Bird
Gareth Stevens editor: Alan Wachtel
Gareth Stevens designer: Scott M. Krall

Photo credits: t–top, c–center, b–bottom, r–right, l–left, The Bridgeman Art Library: Front cover, back cover
(top and bottom), title page, 4t, 4–5b, 5t, 7, 8, 9t, 9b, 11t, 11b, 12l, 12r, 13, 14, 18, 19b, 20, 22, 23, 25b, 29, 31b,
32, 33, 37b, 40, 41, 42, 43, 48, 49, 52, 56, 57, Hulton Getty: 10t, 19t, 31t, 55, Mary Evans Picture Library: 6,
10b, 12t, 16, 17, 21, 24r, 25t, 26, 27, 37t, 38, 46, 51, 53, 59, 60, 61, Novosti: Back cover (center), 15, 24l, 30, 44,
45, 47, 50, 58

Printed in Canada

1 2 3 4 5 6 7 8 9 07 06 05 04 03

CONTENTS

INTRODUCTION

Empress Catherine II, known as Catherine the Great, ruled Russia from 1762 to 1796. Her achievements during those years were impressive. At home, she introduced reforms that changed the lives of everyone, from the poorest serfs to the richest nobles. Abroad, she made Russia a European power that ranked with Austria, Prussia, Britain, and France, while expanding her country's territory both south and west.

This book looks at Catherine and her activities in two different ways. In the first part, you can read the story of her life. It begins with her birth as a minor German princess in 1729 and ends with her death as a mighty Russian empress more than 67 years later. This first part is divided into chapters, and it also includes special features that highlight two subjects, the history of the Romanovs (the Russian imperial family) and the nature of Russian society. In the second part of the book, you can examine more closely the main concerns Catherine dealt with as a leader and her beliefs, policies, and relationships. To help you assess Catherine's ideals and actions for yourself, this part is divided into sections, each headed with an important question to consider. The first two pages in each section provide one possible answer, together with quotations, statistics, and other facts to back it up. The next two pages provide a second potential answer, also with supporting evidence and information.

The question pages can be used in several ways. You may just want to read them through, look at both answers and their supporting evidence, and then make up your own mind about which answer is stronger. Perhaps you could also write down the reasons for your decision.

Catherine the Great walking on the grounds of Tsarskoe Selo, a royal residence, during the final year of her life.

In the 18th century, poor peasants like this girl made up over half the Russian population.

Alternatively, the material can be used in a classroom debate between two groups, each arguing for a different answer. The sources may also inspire further research. You may wish to use the library or the Internet to find more data to back your answers to the questions on which these pages focus.

The question pages have another purpose. They are designed to show you that facts and statistics can be used to support completely different points of view. This is why historians have to sift through a great deal of material from a wide variety of sources before they can reach reliable conclusions about the past. Even then, answers are rarely clear-cut and may be overturned by new evidence. As you consider the questions, remember that neither of the answers provided may be completely correct. Using the information in both parts of the book—and any more you can find—it is up to you to judge for yourself.

RUSSIAN DATES

Until the 16th century, both Russia and Western Europe used the ancient Julian calendar. In 1582, Pope Gregory XIII introduced the Gregorian calendar. This calendar moved the date first 10, then 11, days forward. By Catherine the Great's time, the Gregorian calendar had been adopted in most European countries. Russia, however, kept the Julian calendar until 1918. In this book, Julian dates are used throughout, following the Russian style.

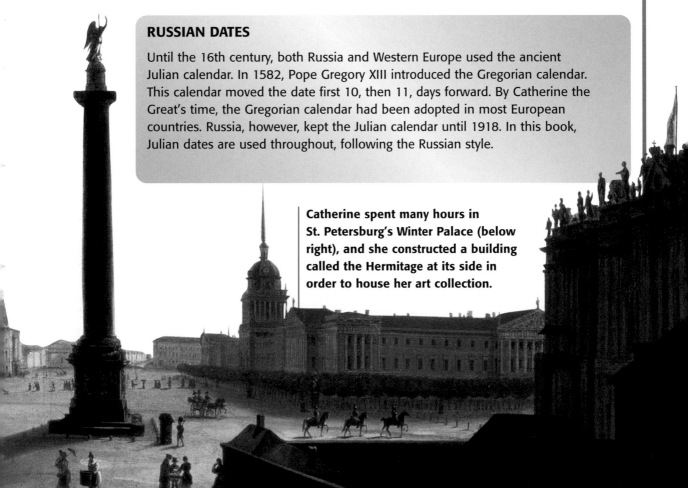

Catherine spent many hours in St. Petersburg's Winter Palace (below right), and she constructed a building called the Hermitage at its side in order to house her art collection.

CHAPTER ONE

EARLY YEARS

In the 18th century, Germany was divided into many states, each with its own ruler. Among these states was the small principality of Anhalt-Zerbst, located in the north of the country. Its ruling family included a prince named Christian August. In 1727, at age 42, he married a princess named Johanna Elizabeth, who was from Holstein-Gottorp, a German state much further to the north.

Christian August was a general in the army of Prussia, a far more important German state than his own. His regiment was based in the town of Stettin, so his wife moved there with him. On April 21, 1729, Johanna Elizabeth, herself only 17, gave birth to their first child, Sophia Augusta Fredericka of Anhalt-Zerbst. Sophia used this name for only 15 years, the years before she started a new life in Russia.

EDUCATION AND ILLNESS

From the age of six, Sophia had a French governess called Babette Cardel, who was a Huguenot refugee. Babette gave the young princess basic reading and spelling lessons, at the same time teaching her the French language and the refined manners of French society. Sophia also had tutors to coach her in special skills, such as dancing, and a priest to instruct her in the beliefs of Lutheranism. She proved to be a spirited, intelligent child who was unafraid to question adults' opinions.

When she was seven, Sophia became seriously ill. She had a severe coughing fit that caused her to fall over, and she developed chest pains and a fever that confined her to bed for three weeks. By the time she was well enough to get up again, her upper body and spine had become misshapen. To correct this condition, the princess had to wear a special brace for about four years. Nevertheless, Sophia continued to be a lively, adventurous, and sometimes argumentative child.

THE WIDER WORLD

Princess Johanna Elizabeth, Sophia's mother, had not grown up in Holstein-Gottorp, the home of her parents. As a child, she had lived

A mid-18th century view of Stettin, the town in which Catherine was born.

This map shows Germany, Poland, and Russia in the mid-18th century. The places mentioned in this chapter are marked.

instead with her godmother in yet another German state, Brunswick-Wolfenbüttel. Court life there was grand and glamorous, and the princess found Stettin very dull by comparison. Happily, Johanna Elizabeth was able to pay regular visits to her godmother in Brunswick, and in 1736, she took her young daughter with her for the first time.

Sophia found this new experience fascinating. She was allowed to stay up late and watch members of royal and aristocratic families from across Europe enjoy themselves at balls and other events. In her memoirs, she recalled that she "chattered like a magpie" with excitement. At the same time, almost without being aware of it happening, the

young princess was learning how to behave among people far grander than any in Stettin. After more trips to Brunswick and other courts—including the Prussian court in Berlin—Sophia gradually began to feel at ease in the wider world.

FIRST LOVE?

Another milestone in Sophia's journey to adulthood took place in 1743, when she was 14. In that year, her mother's 24-year-old

A modern view of Charlottenburg Castle, Berlin, an 18th-century residence of the Prussian court.

brother, Georg-Ludwig, fell desperately in love with Sophia. When he proposed marriage, she was completely astonished. But although she was flattered by his attention, Sophia was unsure of her own feelings. She finally agreed to the match, under the condition that her parents give their consent.

LINKS WITH RUSSIA

Power politics, however, frustrated Georg-Ludwig's desire to marry Sophia. The ruling family of Holstein-Gottorp, to which Sophia's mother belonged, was linked to Russia's imperial family. In 1727, Karl-Friedrich, then the Duke of Holstein-Gottorp, had married Anna Petrovna, who was the daughter of Czar Peter I, known as Peter the Great. A year later, Anna gave birth to a son, Karl Peter Ulrich.

At that time, it seemed unlikely that Karl Peter would ever become Czar of Russia. After Peter the Great died in 1725, first his wife, then members of other branches of his family, ruled the country. The situation began to change in 1740, when Ivan VI came to power. Ivan was only a baby, so his mother, Anna Leopoldovna, ruled on his behalf. In 1741, Peter the Great's second daughter, Elizabeth Petrovna, ordered Anna's arrest. She was thrown into prison with her family, leaving Elizabeth free to take over as empress.

CHOOSING AN HEIR

In order to secure her own position and prevent future unrest, Empress Elizabeth decided to name an heir as soon as possible. She was not married and had no children of her own, so she had to look elsewhere. In 1742, the empress chose the young Karl Peter Ulrich, who by that time had been the ruling Duke of Holstein-Gottorp for three years.

There were several reasons for Elizabeth's choice. First, the Duke's mother, Anna, was her sister. Second, she, Elizabeth, had once been in love with another of the Holstein-Gottorps, a brother of Johanna Elizabeth. He had died, but she remembered him fondly. Finally, she wanted to stop Karl Peter from becoming King of Sweden, a role to which he had a good claim. An alliance between Holstein-Gottorp and Sweden, Russia's old enemy from the Great Northern War and other wars, would have been unwelcome.

Karl Peter Ulrich left Germany for Russia in 1743. Soon after his arrival, he was named Grand Duke and declared heir to the imperial throne. In order to take on these roles, he had to abandon his Lutheran religion for the beliefs and practices of the Russian Orthodox Church. As a sign of this change, he was given a new first name—Peter.

AN ARRANGED MARRIAGE

Johanna Elizabeth, Sophia's mother, was quick to take advantage of Peter's new position. He had already met Sophia, during a visit to the court of Lübeck in 1739. At that time, neither of them had reached their teens, but now they were of marriageable age. Johanna set out to arrange an alliance between Sophia and

Empress Elizabeth had a taste for fine objects. This tankard bears her monogram and enamel pictures of other Russian rulers.

Grand Duke Peter, Catherine's husband, in 1758. He became Czar Peter III in 1761.

promote in Russia. The family then moved on to Stettin, where Christian August remained.

Amid tears and in great secrecy, Sophia and her mother embarked on the final leg of their journey. As the carriage hurried eastward, the temperature steadily fell. Travelling conditions were very unpleasant—Sophia's feet swelled so much that she could not walk. But when the princesses crossed the Polish border into Russia, they were welcomed with great ceremony and given court sleighs in which to continue their journey. Sable furs were provided to keep them warm.

The women made their way first to St. Petersburg, the Russian capital, where many members of the Russian court, though not the Empress Elizabeth, greeted them. Lavish entertainment was provided, but the serious business of betrothal and marriage could not

King Frederick II of Prussia, commonly known as Frederick the Great.

Peter as soon as possible. She made frequent contact with the Russian court and regularly sent them portraits of her blossoming young daughter.

The Empress Elizabeth selected Sophia as Peter's future wife for her own reasons. The young woman's Holstein-Gottorp ancestry in particular made her an acceptable choice. In 1743, the empress sent a letter to Johanna Elizabeth requesting her to visit Russia together with her daughter. Georg-Ludwig's claim on Sophia was immediately swept aside. His older sister already had her eyes on the glittering Russian throne.

JOURNEY TO RUSSIA

Sophia's father, Christian August, doubted the wisdom of her trip to Russia, but in early 1744, the whole family set out from Anhalt-Zerbst. Their first stop was in Berlin, where they visited Frederick II, King of Prussia. He instructed Johanna Elizabeth in Prussian foreign policy aims, which he wanted her to

The Winter Palace as it appeared when Catherine arrived in St. Petersburg. By 1762, a new palace had been built on the same site.

wait long. The Empress and Grand Duke Peter were expecting Sophia and her mother in Moscow. Johanna Elizabeth was advised to reach the city before February 10, the date of her future son-in-law's birthday.

MEETING IN MOSCOW

The princesses arrived on the outskirts of Moscow on February 9. At nightfall, they made their way to the Annenhof Palace, where the court was assembled. Grand Duke Peter made his entrance at about 10 o'clock, and then the entire company proceeded through the state apartments to see Empress Elizabeth. She dismissed them after only a brief audience, but the Grand Duke entertained the new arrivals for the rest of the evening.

During the days that followed, Peter and Sophia became more closely acquainted. It soon became clear to the princess that the Grand Duke was immature and had poor judgment.

In particular, his failure to conceal his preference for Germany and Lutheranism over Russia and the Orthodox Church seemed to her highly unwise. She, by contrast, was determined to embrace wholeheartedly the new society in which she found herself. So she applied her great strength of will and intelligence to the study of Russian and the beliefs of the Orthodox church.

Sophia had been in Russia less than two weeks when she fell ill once more. For a month it seemed that she might die, but by April 21, 1744, her 15th birthday, she had recovered. The Empress Elizabeth was by then very fond of Sophia, but she distrusted her mother, Johanna Elizabeth. On the instructions of King Frederick II of Prussia, Johanna Elizabeth had plotted against the anti-Prussian Vice-Chancellor (later Chancellor) of Russia, Count Aleksei Bestuzhev-Riumin. The plot was discovered and Johanna Elizabeth was disgraced.

An 18th-century bishop of the Russian Orthodox church in his elaborate robes.

CONVERSION AND MARRIAGE

Despite these distractions, plans for Sophia and Peter's wedding continued. But before it could go ahead, the princess had to convert to Russian Orthodoxy. This took place during a ceremony in Moscow on June 28, 1744. At this time, Sophia was renamed Catherine. The next day, she and 16-year-old Grand Duke Peter were officially engaged to be married.

The intelligent and vivacious Catherine did not find her future husband to be a very stimulating companion, but his looks were passable. In late 1744, however, Peter developed smallpox. The sores caused by the disease eventually disappeared, but they left his face deeply scarred and swollen, making him physically unattractive to Catherine. Nevertheless, in June 1745, the couple's much-anticipated wedding was arranged for August 21 of the same year.

The wedding took place in the Church of the Virgin of Kazan in St. Petersburg. The pomp and splendor of the festivities could not remove the many doubts in the bride's mind. In her memoirs, she later recalled thinking to herself: "If you allow yourself to love that man, you will be the unhappiest creature on this Earth . . . this man scarcely looks at you, talks of nothing but dolls or such things, and pays more attention to any other woman than yourself." The omens for the young couple's future were not good.

A portrait of the young Catherine, probably painted in 1745, the year of her marriage to Grand Duke Peter.

A view of the Church of the Virgin of Kazan (Kazan Cathedral) in St. Petersburg, where Catherine and Peter were married.

THE ROMANOV DYNASTY

Catherine married into the Romanov dynasty of Russian rulers. This dynasty began in 1613 when Mikhail Feodorovich Romanov became czar. He had inherited the name from his great-aunt, Anastasia Romanov, wife of 16th-century czar Ivan IV, known as "Ivan the Terrible." Mikhail's reign brought relative calm after the 15-year "Time of Troubles," during which rivals had fought for the throne. Romanovs then remained in power for 300 years and made the Russian Empire the largest in the world. The last Romanov, Nicholas II, abdicated in 1917, as the Russian Revolution began. Many of the greatest Romanovs, including Catherine herself, ruled Russia from the late 17th to the late 18th century. The simplified family tree on the right includes all these men and women, as well as their immediate relatives. Reign dates appear below rulers' names. The brief biographies below provide some more details about some of the czars and empresses whose lives affected Catherine the Great.

Czar Mikhail Feodorovich Romanov

PETER THE GREAT (ABOVE)

Peter the Great, or Peter I, was the grandson of the first Romanov, Mikhail. In 1682, at the age of 10, he shared power with his disabled half brother Ivan V. From 1689, he ruled alone, although Ivan did not die until 1696.

Peter used his great energies to modernize Russia and make it a major European power. As a first step he created the Russian navy, which defeated the Turks in 1696. Then, in 1697, he set out on a trip across Europe to investigate every aspect of Western technology, from shipbuilding to clock making. When he returned in 1698, he brought with him about 900 craftspeople to introduce European skills to Russia.

From 1700 to 1721, Peter waged the Great Northern War against Sweden for control of territory around the Baltic Sea. In 1703, he began to build the city of St. Petersburg on captured land. Nine years later, this city replaced Moscow as Russia's capital. The war ended in victory and expansion for Russia; this was the start of the Russian Empire, and it allowed Peter to adopt the title "Emperor and Autocrat of All Russia."

Peter's achievements at home were also immense. He reformed Russia's administration and army, and he encouraged education and trade. He also curbed the power of the nobles and the Orthodox Church by bringing them under state control. Peter died in 1725. His life and ideals were later an inspiration to Catherine the Great.

CATHERINE I (ABOVE)

Catherine I was a Lithuanian peasant who was originally named Marfa Skavronskaya. She adopted the name Catherine after joining the Russian Orthodox Church. In 1703, Peter the Great took Catherine as his lover, having divorced his first wife in 1698. Four years later, the couple

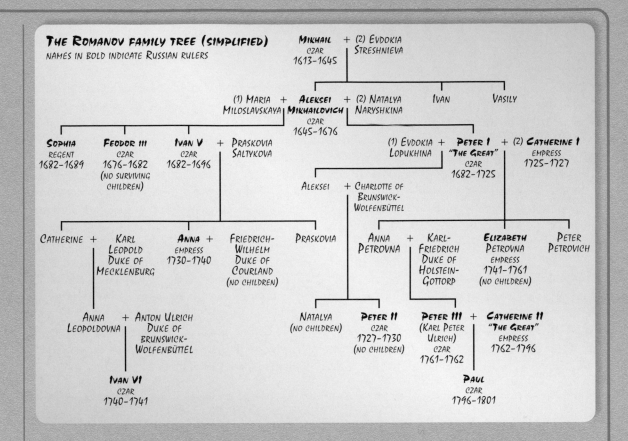

The Romanov family tree (simplified)
NAMES IN BOLD INDICATE RUSSIAN RULERS

MIKHAIL
CZAR
1613–1645
+ (2) EVDOKIA STRESHNIEVA

(1) MARIA MILOSLAVSKAYA + **ALEKSEI MIKHAILOVICH** CZAR 1645–1676 + (2) NATALYA NARYSHKINA   IVAN   VASILY

SOPHIA REGENT 1682–1689

FEODOR III CZAR 1676–1682 (NO SURVIVING CHILDREN)

IVAN V CZAR 1682–1696 + PRASKOVIA SALTYKOVA

(1) EVDOKIA LOPUKHINA + **PETER I "THE GREAT"** CZAR 1682–1725 + (2) **CATHERINE I** EMPRESS 1725–1727

ALEKSEI + CHARLOTTE OF BRUNSWICK-WOLFENBÜTTEL

CATHERINE + KARL LEOPOLD DUKE OF MECKLENBURG

ANNA EMPRESS 1730–1740 + FRIEDRICH-WILHELM DUKE OF COURLAND (NO CHILDREN)

PRASKOVIA

ANNA PETROVNA + KARL-FRIEDRICH DUKE OF HOLSTEIN-GOTTORP

ELIZABETH PETROVNA EMPRESS 1741–1761 (NO CHILDREN)

PETER PETROVICH

ANNA LEOPOLDOVNA + ANTON ULRICH DUKE OF BRUNSWICK-WOLFENBÜTTEL

NATALYA (NO CHILDREN)

PETER II CZAR 1727–1730 (NO CHILDREN)

PETER III (KARL PETER ULRICH) CZAR 1761–1762 + **CATHERINE II "THE GREAT"** EMPRESS 1762–1796

IVAN VI CZAR 1740–1741

PAUL CZAR 1796–1801

---

married secretly. A public wedding followed in 1712. Together, they had 12 children, including Anna, mother of Catherine the Great's husband, Peter III, and Elizabeth, who preceded him as empress. Peter the Great failed to name an heir before his death in 1725, but as Catherine I had the support of the elite Preobrazhensky Guards, she was proclaimed empress. Her main political achievement was to establish the Supreme Privy Council in 1726. It remained Russia's most powerful government body until 1730. Catherine I died of a fever in 1727.

IVAN VI
Ivan VI became emperor in 1740, when he was less than two months old. A year later, Ivan and his mother, Anna, were overthrown in a coup led by the future Empress Elizabeth. He and his whole family were imprisoned for three years before they were exiled to the far north. When his mother died in 1746, Ivan was placed in solitary confinement. His mere existence, however, was a threat to Elizabeth because many people believed he had a better claim to the throne than she did. In 1756, she moved him to a fortress in a place called Schlüsselburg. Ivan's guards were told to kill him if any escape attempt took place. Catherine the Great gave them the same order, for the same reason, when she took power in 1762. Just two years later, when a soldier tried to free the former czar, his guards stabbed Ivan VI to death.

ELIZABETH (ABOVE)
Elizabeth seized power from Ivan VI in 1741. Physically, she was a model empress—majestic and strikingly beautiful. Much of her life was devoted to dancing and other entertainments, but she also played an important political role. Elizabeth led Russia to victory in a two-year war against Sweden that ended in 1743. She also took Russia into two conflicts in Western Europe, the War of the Austrian Succession (1740–1748) and the Seven Years' War (1756–1763). Russian troops did not, in fact, fight in the first war, but along with Austria, they scored major victories against Prussia in the Seven Years' War. In 1760, the Russians occupied Prussia's capital, Berlin. By that time, Elizabeth had suffered two strokes. She died from a third stroke in 1761. Her successor, Catherine the Great's husband, Peter III, took Russian foreign policy in a totally different direction.

A MARRIED WOMAN

The Empress Elizabeth wanted Catherine to produce an heir as soon as possible. But as far as historians are able to judge, the newly married princess remained a virgin long after her wedding night. For Catherine, this private disappointment combined with a more public sorrow when her mother returned to Germany. Just 16 years old and married to an uncaring husband, she now found herself friendless in a foreign land.

FEAR AND SUSPICION

Catherine's situation steadily worsened. Her failure to become pregnant—through no fault of her own—led the empress to grow suspicious. Elizabeth feared that Catherine was forming unsuitable relationships with men other than her husband or even plotting against Russia on behalf of Prussia. Urged on by Count Aleksei Bestuzhev-Riumin, she therefore decided to take total control of Catherine's life.

In May 1746, Empress Elizabeth put Maria Semenovna Choglokov in charge of Catherine's household. A married cousin of the empress's, Maria was to spy on Catherine and to provide an example of correct wifely behavior. Catherine's freedom was also limited in several other ways. In particular, she was forbidden to send any letters that

The Catherine Palace in Tsarskoe Selo. A royal residence in Catherine the Great's time, it was named after Catherine I.

had not first been checked by the Foreign Office. Furthermore, she was no longer allowed to speak quietly to servants, in case she was hatching a plot.

Catherine's husband, the Grand Duke Peter, was also closely watched. Nevertheless, his life contained many pleasures. He loved to play with toy soldiers, to breed dogs, to drink, and to indulge in wild horseplay. Although he was unable or unwilling to have a child with Catherine, he did, however, gossip to her for hours. She found his chatter tedious and preferred to fill the long days with reading and horseback riding.

SERGEI SALTYKOV

Catherine's life continued in this aimless fashion for years. The death of her father in 1747 caused her great sorrow, even more so because she was not allowed to mourn him properly. Otherwise, the main events that punctuated her quiet existence were the journeys she made from Moscow to St. Petersburg and back. (It was customary for the imperial family to live in different palaces during different seasons of the year.) Meanwhile, she was growing into an attractive woman. Her husband, however, remained indifferent.

Many other men were not indifferent, however, and in 1752, one of them began to court her. He was Sergei Saltykov, a charming, handsome 26-year-old chamberlain to Grand Duke Peter. Although he was married, Saltykov pursued the 23-year-old Catherine relentlessly. At first, she tried to resist, but loneliness made her vulnerable. Eventually the two became lovers.

A SON AND HEIR

Before the year's end, Catherine found herself pregnant. She miscarried and continued her relationship with Saltykov. By this time, the affair was supported by both Count Bestuzhev-Riumin and Maria Choglokov, probably with the knowledge of the Empress Elizabeth. The pressing need—seven years after Catherine and Peter's marriage—was for an heir. The question of who the father was, provided his identity remained a secret, had become less important.

Eventually, following a second miscarriage, Catherine gave birth to a son on September 20, 1754. He was named Paul Petrovich Romanov, and he immediately became second in line for the Russian throne. Although it is possible that Catherine's husband was Paul's father, most historians believe his father was Saltykov. The empress was delighted with the baby and decided to bring him up herself. She took him from Catherine to live in her own apartments, leaving his mother desolate.

STANISLAUS PONIATOWSKI

Catherine soon faced more misery. Saltykov ended their affair shortly after Paul's birth. Meanwhile, her husband had taken a mistress whom he did not bother to hide. At first, Catherine consoled herself by reading works by French writers; Charles de Montesquieu and Voltaire were among her favorites. But then she began another relationship.

Catherine the Great's son, Paul Petrovich Romanov, as a boy. He eventually ruled Russia as Czar Paul from 1796 to 1801.

15

A Married Woman

In the 18th century, Russia was often courted by rival European powers seeking it as an ally. Among them was Britain, which sent a new ambassador to St. Petersburg in 1755. The new ambassador, Charles Hanbury-Williams, was accompanied by Count Stanislaus Poniatowski, a 23-year-old Pole. The count had lived in England and France, had read widely, and spoke several languages. Catherine was instantly attracted to the cultured young noble. Soon, the two were in love.

Catherine's personal happiness developed at a time when major political changes were taking place in Russia and abroad. In June 1756, the 46-year-old Empress Elizabeth had a stroke. At once, the thoughts of the Russian people turned to the question of her successor. Some believed the empress might disinherit the Grand Duke Peter, for whom she had little respect, in favor of Catherine's son, Paul. Meanwhile, war was looming in Europe.

The Seven Years' War

The major European states—France, Austria, Prussia, and Britain—had long been in conflict over land and power. Alliances between them shifted according to need and opportunity, and the different alliances often sought Russian backing. At the Empress Elizabeth's court, there were two rival foreign-policy factions. One, led by Elizabeth's chancellor, Count Bestuzhev-Riumin, favored supporting Britain and Austria against France and Prussia. The other, led by Vice-Chancellor Mikhail Vorontsov, worked for closer Russian ties with France.

Stanislaus Poniatowski, Catherine's second lover. This image shows him after he became King of Poland in 1764.

In 1755, Russia had signed an agreement with Britain under which the two countries pledged to together oppose Prussia in war. Count Bestuzhev-Riumin was content. But a year later, in 1756, Britain made an alliance with Prussia. This led to a deep sense of betrayal in Russia and to the discrediting of Bestuzhev-Riumin. The new British-Prussian alliance also prompted two other former enemies, France and Austria, to join in a new coalition. Russia, where the pro-French faction now had the upper hand, was poised to become its third member.

In August 1756, King Frederick II of Prussia invaded Saxony, a small German state that supported Austria. This invasion was the start of the Seven Years' War. For several months, Count Bestuzhev-Riumin, together with the British ambassador, Sir Charles Hanbury-Williams, struggled to stop Russia from allying itself with Austria and France. They were aided by Catherine, who was already secretly working with them to ensure that her son Paul would become Russia's emperor on the death of Elizabeth.

But all their efforts were in vain. On December 31, 1756, Elizabeth joined the Franco-Austrian alliance, and in May of the

A 1760 scene from the Seven Years' War, during which an alliance of Austria, France, and Russia fought Britain and Prussia. Here, the Prussians are defeating the Austrians.

following year, Russian troops invaded Prussia. In July, Hanbury-Williams returned to Britain, Prussia's main ally in the war. A month later, the Russians won a great victory against the Prussians at Gross-Jägerndorf.

A LUCKY ESCAPE

In September 1757, Empress Elizabeth had a second stroke. Now, in the middle of a war against Prussia, it appeared that the pro-Prussian Grand Duke Peter might accede to the throne. Elizabeth, however, recovered and responded angrily to the news that Field Marshal Apraksin, who was the commander of Russia's forces in Prussia, had pulled his men back. She suspected, probably wrongly, that Bestuzhev-Riumin had encouraged him to do so. In 1758, she had the Chancellor arrested.

Catherine now found herself in a dangerous position. She realized that if her letters to Bestuzhev-Riumin were found, her involvement in political intrigue, already suspected, would become clear. The Chancellor had, in fact, burned almost all the papers likely to incriminate her, but she did not know this.

Catherine could only wait and hope. Later, after two highly charged meetings with the empress, Catherine's innocence was accepted. Bestuzhev-Riumin was not so fortunate; he was exiled in disgrace.

AN END AND A BEGINNING

Catherine had intermittently continued her affair with Stanislaus Poniatowski. In 1756, she gave birth to another child, Anna Petrovna, who was probably fathered by Poniatowski. Because there was a suggestion that he, too, was involved in the Bestuzhev-Riumin scandal, Poniatowski was sent back to Poland in 1758. The relationship was over.

In 1759, Russian forces won a second major victory over the Prussian army, at Künersdorf. The next year, they and the Austrians briefly occupied Berlin. Prussia fought back hard but by 1761 was on the brink of defeat. Catherine, meanwhile, was

This 19th-century painting shows Catherine (in the red sash) arriving to view Empress Elizabeth's body in its coffin before burial.

Grigory Orlov was one of five brothers who belonged to Guards regiments. They were all known for their bravery and love of women.

beginning a third affair. This time her partner was Grigory Orlov, a dashing Russian Guards officer.

A NEW RULER

By now, the Empress Elizabeth was visibly fading. She found it hard to walk or even breathe. On December 23, 1761, she was laid low by a third stroke, and she died on Christmas Day. Catherine's husband was immediately proclaimed Czar Peter III. Fortunately, the reign of this childish man—who showed open contempt

Catherine gave birth in 1762 to a son fathered by Grigory Orlov. This painting shows the boy, Aleksei Bobrinskoi, as a seven-year-old.

for his Russian subjects, their Orthodox religion, and almost everything else they held dear—was to be short-lived.

Despite all his inadequacies, Peter III did introduce some reforms. He reorganized the government and filled it with his own friends and family, many of them German. He abolished the Secret Chancery, an institution that had rooted out treason through intimidation and torture. He freed the nobility from compulsory state service and gave them more control over their serfs. He also greatly reduced the Orthodox Church's power, in particular by starting to bring its land under state control.

These reforms made Peter some friends and many enemies, especially among former government officials and the clergy. His fatal mistake, however, was to alienate the army. The army was riding high after the successes against Prussia, and it was ready to seize the final victory. But almost as soon as he became czar, the pro-Prussian Peter declared his intention to begin peace talks. They were concluded in April 1762, and their terms included the return to Prussia of all the land Russia had won in the war.

As if this humiliation were not enough, Peter also reorganized the Russian army in the Prussian style. Then, in May 1762, he launched a war against Denmark that was purely for the benefit of Holstein-Gottorp, the German state from which he came. Russian troops were expected to fight alongside Prussians, their official allies, for a cause in which they had no interest. Rage against the czar became widespread. Catherine, who had recently given birth to a son fathered by Orlov, was ready and waiting in the wings.

THE NEW EMPRESS

Peter III's reign ended swiftly and without violence. Early on the morning of June 28, 1762, Catherine and Aleksei Orlov, brother of Grigory, made their way into St. Petersburg by carriage. Grigory rode alongside the carriage. Once in the city, Catherine was publicly proclaimed empress at the barracks of the Izmailovsky Guards.

There followed a triumphant procession through the streets, with the new Catherine II in her carriage at its center. The new empress first visited the barracks of other Guards regiments, where she received their allegiance. Next she went to the Church of the Virgin of Kazan, where the Archbishop of Novgorod blessed her in her new role. Finally, she entered the Winter Palace, where she broke the news to her son, Paul.

TWO MURDERS

At first, the former Czar Peter, who was away in Oranienbaum, was unaware of the momentous events taking place. But when the truth became clear, it was too late to resist. He was

In this famous painting, Catherine is shown dressed in a Guards uniform leading out troops to arrest her husband.

Catherine the Great's coronation took place on September 22, 1762, in the Cathedral of the Assumption, located in Moscow.

forced to sign an unconditional abdication, and he was then moved to the country estate of Ropsha and kept under house arrest. Soon after, on July 6, he died. The official cause of death was listed as colic resulting from hemorrhoids. Others blamed a drunken fight. Most historians, however, now believe that Peter was murdered by Aleksei Orlov.

The extent of Catherine's involvement in Peter's murder is open to debate. Whatever the truth, his death strengthened her hold on the Russian throne. At the same time, there remained two other people with a greater right to rule. One was her son, Paul. Catherine herself had once hoped to make him czar in her husband's place. The boy, however, was only eight years old, so for the time being, at least, he did not pose a major threat. The other was former czar Ivan VI, now in his 20s.

His murder in Schlüsselburg in 1764 put an end to his claim.

TAKING CONTROL

Empress Catherine II was ambitious, but she was not interested in power for its own sake. She had serious plans for her adopted country that had been shaped both by wide reading and deep thought.

In the first two years of her reign, Catherine set up commissions to examine existing policies. One commission reviewed Peter III's confiscation of church land, a process that was ultimately completed. Another investigated the former czar's unpopular changes to the army, which were replaced by far more acceptable reforms. A third commission considered how best to develop Russian trade.

Another important commission had a dual purpose. It was set up in February 1763 to debate the role of the nobles, and, in particular, the new freedoms granted to them by Peter III. Starting in April of the same year, this commission also began to review the Senate, Russia's main central government institution. In December, Catherine issued an *ukaz*, or decree that reformed the Senate.

POWER AND PROTEST

Her reign gathered momentum in 1764. In February, Catherine finally took all church lands under state control. In July, she set up a government department to encourage foreign settlement in Russia. As a result, German colonies grew up around the Volga river. Also in July, the empress confirmed the alliance with Prussia that her husband had made in 1762. In August, she and Frederick II acted to ensure that Poniatowski, once her lover, became king of Poland.

Apart from these great public events, Catherine continued to address the problem of peasant unrest. Back in 1762, about 200,000 serfs and other peasants had been in open revolt. The empress sent envoys to deal with particular local difficulties, set up commissions, and introduced new regulations. The turmoil persisted, but Catherine was determined to find a solution. In 1765, she supported the creation of the Free Economic Society. Its members were interested in the question of whether the role of the Russian peasants should be totally reformed.

THE LEGISLATIVE COMMISSION AND THE BOLSHOI NAKAZ

Catherine firmly believed that she, as empress, should have absolute power. At the same time, she considered it her duty to use this power wisely, for the good of all her subjects. She had come to this conclusion largely

These charming pottery figures of a peasant couple and an Orthodox priest (right) were made in 18th-century Russia.

as a result of reading works by thinkers of the Enlightenment, an important intellectual movement of the 18th century.

Catherine's great dream was to reform Russia's legal code, the *Ulozhenie*, according to her Enlightenment principles. The code dated from 1649, and many of its laws—there were more than 10,000—were bad for or irrelevant to life in the 18th century. Catherine wanted nothing less than a total overhaul. In 1766, she called for the establishment of a Legislative Commission to undertake this work.

By this time, the empress had begun to prepare an extraordinary document. The *Bolshoi Nakaz*, or "Great Instruction," detailed her beliefs about everything from good government to the practice of religion. It drew heavily on the works of the Enlightenment thinkers Cesare Beccaria and Charles de Montesquieu, and many of its 526 (later 655) numbered paragraphs were true to Enlightenment ideals. The document made clear, however, that the empress considered autocracy the only possible way in which Russia could be effectively governed.

In spring 1767, Catherine made an official trip to Russia's Volga river region. In July, after she had returned, the first version of the *Bolshoi Nakaz* was published. It was then sent around the country and abroad, where it gained high praise from the Enlightenment writer Voltaire. Publication of the document coincided with the first meeting of the new

Legislative Commission, located in Moscow's Kremlin. Copies of the empress's document were presented to the 564 delegates from all over Russia, with the intention that it should guide their debates.

COLLAPSE OF THE COMMISSION

The composition of the Legislative Commission was extremely varied. As well as members of the Senate, the Synod, and other government bodies, it contained elected nobles, townspeople, peasants, Cossacks, and members of non-Russian tribes such as the Kalmyks. All serfs, however, were excluded. Divided by rank, wealth, place of origin, and religion—Muslims and pagans mingled with the Orthodox Christian majority—the delegates found it extremely hard to establish any common ground.

There were other problems. Although most delegates admired the high-minded ideals expressed in the *Bolshoi Nakaz*, they could not connect them with their daily lives. Some groups, particularly the nobles, were concerned more with the preservation of their own privileges than with the establishment of a just society. There was also a reluctance among the delegates to speak freely about some issues for fear of causing offense.

In October 1768, the empress was briefly distracted from the dealings of the Legislative Commission when she had herself inoculated against smallpox by English doctor Thomas Dimsdale. Her aim was to encourage her subjects to do likewise, and the Senate gave her twelve gold medals for bravery. By the end of the year, however, it was clear the commission would never achieve its purpose. In December, after 17 months and 200 meetings, the commission was dissolved. By then, Catherine had already turned her attention to problems beyond Russia's borders.

CATHERINE AND THE ENLIGHTENMENT

The thinkers and writers of the 18th-century movement known as the Enlightenment set out to investigate and explain the world using not the old tools of religion and tradition, but the new tools of reason and science. In their view, superstition—by which they generally meant the beliefs of the Church—and lack of rational education were responsible for many of society's ills. They aimed to bring the light of knowledge into every area of life, from politics to law. Their motto was "Dare to know!"

Many of the greatest Enlightenment thinkers came from France. They included Charles de Montesquieu, whose masterpiece *Spirit of the Laws* (1748) analyzed different types of governments and greatly inspired Catherine II as she prepared the *Bolshoi Nakaz*. Equally influential was another French writer, Voltaire (left), whose real name was François Marie Arouet. He and the empress exchanged letters for many years.

Another of Catherine's Enlightenment mentors was Cessare Beccaria, an Italian. His *Essay on Crimes and Punishments* (1764) argued against the use of torture and the death penalty. Beccaria's influence on the *Bolshoi Nakaz* is clear. For example, in paragraph 123, it states "The Usage of Torture is contrary to all the Dictates of Nature and Reason. . . ."

RUSSIAN SOCIETY

From the foundation of the first true Russian state in the 9th century A.D., Russian society was arranged in a complex hierarchy, with rulers and nobles at the top and peasants at the bottom. By the 17th century, there was a bewildering array of about 500 social categories. The precise status, rights, and duties of each, however, was not legally defined. Under the Romanovs, this situation changed.

Each of the sections below describes how one major social grouping in Russia, known as an estate, developed from the mid-17th century to the time of Catherine the Great and beyond. The information about these social groups will help you understand the background to, and sometimes also the direct causes of, many of the major historical events that are described in the pages of this book.

SERFS

Until the mid-17th century, Russian peasants who worked on private estates enjoyed some rights, including the right to move to other estates and work for other landowners. Even when they left an estate illegally, there was a time limit for their recovery. If their landlords did not catch them within five years, they were free. But in 1649, Romanov czar Aleksei Mikhailovich introduced the *Ulozhenie* legal code, the measures of which included the legal establishment of serfdom.

Under this code, serfs had almost no rights. They were tied to one landlord, who effectively owned them. They could be bought and sold like animals, and if they ran away, their landlords had a permanent right to recapture them. Life for the serfs was harsh. In many areas, the Russian soil was poor and hard to work. From the little they owned, serfs had to give their landlords *obrok,* or payment in the form of money, goods, or both, for the use of land. Often, they also had to carry out *barshchina*, or compulsory labor, in the landlords' fields. From 1718, they also had to pay a state poll tax. The grim conditions endured by serfs led to the revolts that were a constant feature of Catherine the Great's reign.

STATE PEASANTS AND COSSACKS

More than half the peasants in Russia were privately owned serfs. There were also many thousands of state peasants, who lived and worked on state-owned land. Their numbers were boosted after 1764, when church lands and the peasants who worked

A Cossack on horseback.

them were taken over by the state government.

Like serfs, state peasants paid *obrok* and poll taxes. In contrast to serfs, they had many more rights, and they were allowed to participate in the Legislative Commission.

The Cossacks were originally independent bands of warrior horsemen that included many escaped serfs. During the 18th century, however, they came under closer state control and were forced to pay the poll tax. As a result, they became a type of state peasant. Many Cossacks deeply resented this change. One Cossack, Emelyan Pugachev, led the most serious rebellion against Catherine the Great's reign.

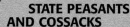

18th-century Russian peasants.

NOBLES

In the early 17th century, there were three main groups of Russian nobles, of which the highest-ranking were the boyars. The majority came from old-established noble families, which monopolized the top military and state posts. Czar Peter the Great overhauled this system by publishing the Table of Ranks in 1722. It divided service at court, in the armed forces, and in the civil administration into fourteen *chiny*, or ranks. Access was open not only to hereditary nobles but also to nonnobles, who could gain noble status by reaching a certain rank.

Peter the Great expected life service from nobles, but later rulers were less demanding. Empress Anna, who reigned from 1730 to 1740, reduced the requirement to twenty-five years.

A group of boyars.

Peter III abolished compulsory service altogether. In her Charter to the Nobles of 1785, Catherine the Great divided Russia's nobles into six groups and legally defined their rights. These rights included the right to shun service at court, but nobles who took this option were not allowed to participate in local government.

TOWNSPEOPLE

Many peasants and nobles lived in towns, but they were not classified as townspeople, that is, official members of the urban estate. The 1649 *Ulozhenie* defined this group as people who practiced a trade or skill in a town. They included a wide variety of Russians, from rich merchants to poor craftspeople. Townspeople had to pay several taxes, including the poll tax. Their freedom of movement was limited. Merchants, for example, needed a special passport before they were allowed to leave their own towns to sell goods.

In the early 18th century, Peter the Great stimulated the development of Russian towns by restructuring urban social groups and encouraging craft guilds. The reforms had only limited success. Catherine later made a major attempt to reorganize urban areas in her 1785 Charter to the Towns. From that time on, townspeople, like the country's nobles, were also divided into six groups.

A town merchant and his family.

CHAPTER FOUR

WAR, REBELLION, AND REFORM

In the 1770 Battle of Chesmé, Russian ships sank the Ottoman fleet while it was anchored in the Aegean Sea, between Greece and Turkey.

To the country's southwest, Russia was bordered by the vast Muslim empire of the Ottoman Turks. By the time Catherine became empress, there had been several wars between the two powers over territory. In particular, Russia coveted several ports on the Black Sea that were under Turkish power. In 1768, fighting began again.

THE FIRST TURKISH WAR

The immediate cause of the First Turkish War was the situation in Poland. The country, now ruled by Catherine's former lover, Stanislaus Poniatowski, was heavily under Russian influence. Most Poles, however, were Roman Catholics, and they denied members of the Orthodox Church—the church of Russia—and Protestants their political rights. In 1764, Catherine, backed by Frederick II of Prussia and aided by her new foreign policy

adviser, Nikita Panin, set out to enforce religious equality in Poland.

Her actions served only to anger patriotic Polish nobles. By 1768, a full-scale rebellion was under way. On the empress's orders, Russian troops invaded Poland and quelled the revolt. When the Russians seemed in no hurry to leave Poland, the Turks objected to the continuing Russian presence on their northern border. Tension increased after Cossacks pursued Polish rebels over the border and onto Turkish soil. In October 1768, when a final demand for Russia to leave Poland was not met, the Turks declared war.

Russian troops moved south into the Crimea and west into the Balkans, capturing

Bucharest and pushing the Turks across the Danube River. Then, in 1770, Aleksei Orlov led Russia's fleet to a stunning victory at the Battle of Chesmé, in the Aegean Sea. By now, however, Austria was growing wary of the Russian advance towards its territory. Prussia also wanted to hold Russia back. So Frederick II suggested a solution.

PARTITION AND PEACE

The king's idea was to persuade the Austrian rulers, Empress Maria Theresa and Emperor Joseph II, against joining the war on the Turkish side by offering them a large slice of Polish territory. Russia would also take a part of Poland in return for handing lands close to Austria back to Turkey, and Prussia would take a third part of Poland for resolving the problem. This scheme, known as the First Partition, was put into effect in 1772. Poland lost about a third of its land and about half of its people.

By this time, peace talks with the Turks were under way, but no agreement could be reached. Russia, therefore, continued its military campaigns, and by 1773, Constantinople, the Turkish capital, was in danger. Now the Turks were forced to come to terms, and in July 1774, they signed the Treaty of Kutchuk Kainardji. Russia made some major gains, including a section of the Black Sea coast and the right for its ships to sail across the sea and on into the Mediterranean. Turkey recovered its Balkan lands, but the formerly Turkish Crimea was made independent.

SORROW AND CELEBRATION

While Russian troops were engaged abroad, Catherine was kept busy at home. In August 1771, plague struck Moscow. The empress sent her lover, Grigory Orlov, to contain the epidemic. By December, it was under control. About 100,000 people, however, had died.

In September 1773, Catherine's son, Paul, married Wilhelmina of Hesse-Darmstadt, the daughter of a German landgrave, or count.

Like the empress before her, Wilhelmina accepted the Orthodox faith and adopted a new name, Natalya Alekseyevna. Catherine, however, was not able to celebrate the wedding and the promise of an heir for long.

THE PUGACHEV REVOLT

Serf rebellions often erupted in Russia, but they were generally suppressed without difficulty. However, on September 17, 1773, a Cossack named Emelyan Pugachev launched a revolt in the south of the country that caused the authorities serious concern.

Pugachev, who claimed to be Catherine's dead husband, Peter III, rallied different groups of supporters to his cause by offering them exactly what they wanted. To his fellow Cossacks, for example, he promised the renewal of former privileges, while to the serfs he held out the hope of emancipation. His tactics worked well and the revolt spread

Emelyan Pugachev caged and in chains before his execution. About 10,000 rebels died during the revolt that he led.

quickly. Soon about 200,000 men and women were rampaging across the land, killing, burning, and even capturing cities such as Kazan.

The official response was at first hampered by the fact that many troops were away fighting the Turks. Once back, however, they went in hard, defeating the rebels in August 1774. Pugachev was betrayed by his former supporters, carried to Moscow in a cage, and tried. In 1775, he was beheaded and dismembered. After the revolt, Catherine cut Cossack privileges further and increased the number of military bases across Russia.

LOCAL GOVERNMENT REFORM

The speed with which the Pugachev Revolt spread across Russia highlighted the failings of the country's local government system. Peter the Great had reformed the system, dividing the land into huge *gubernii,* or provinces, which were in turn divided into subprovinces and smaller *uezdy,* or districts. As early as 1764, Catherine had decided to further his work. After the Pugachev Revolt, she began in earnest. The Statute for the Administration of the Provinces was passed in 1775. Its main measures included the redrawing of province boundaries so that each contained 300,000 to 400,000 people and the redrawing of district boundaries so that districts each had 20,000 to 30,000. The intermediate subprovinces were abolished.

Catherine appointed a governor to run each of the 50 new provinces. These men, who were responsible to the central government, worked with the aid of local government boards. Every province also had a Treasury Chamber to deal with finance, and a Board of Social Welfare to run institutions such as schools, hospitals, and asylums. The

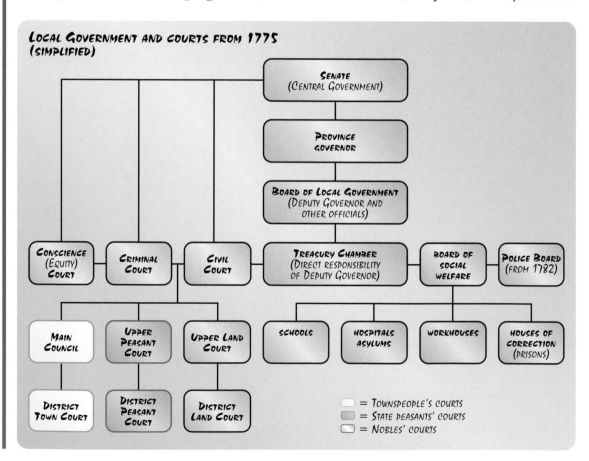

LOCAL GOVERNMENT AND COURTS FROM 1775 (SIMPLIFIED)

SENATE (CENTRAL GOVERNMENT)

PROVINCE GOVERNOR

BOARD OF LOCAL GOVERNMENT (DEPUTY GOVERNOR AND OTHER OFFICIALS)

CONSCIENCE (EQUITY) COURT — CRIMINAL COURT — CIVIL COURT — TREASURY CHAMBER (DIRECT RESPONSIBILITY OF DEPUTY GOVERNOR) — BOARD OF SOCIAL WELFARE — POLICE BOARD (FROM 1782)

MAIN COUNCIL — UPPER PEASANT COURT — UPPER LAND COURT — SCHOOLS — HOSPITALS ASYLUMS — WORKHOUSES — HOUSES OF CORRECTION (PRISONS)

DISTRICT TOWN COURT — DISTRICT PEASANT COURT — DISTRICT LAND COURT

☐ = TOWNSPEOPLE'S COURTS
☐ = STATE PEASANTS' COURTS
☐ = NOBLES' COURTS

PRINCESS TARAKANOVA

While dealing with both the Pugachev Revolt and the Turkish War, Catherine the Great had to face a third problem. News reached her that a beautiful young woman was traveling around Europe falsely claiming to be the daughter of the former Empress Elizabeth and so Russia's true ruler. At Catherine's request, Aleksei Orlov had the woman kidnapped and imprisoned in the Peter and Paul Fortress in St. Petersburg. She died there, probably of consumption, in 1775. The woman called herself by many false names but is generally now known as Princess Tarakanova, a name she herself never in fact used.

Grigory Potemkin. His romantic relationship with Catherine ended in 1776, but he remained a trusted friend until his death.

1782 Police Code added a Police Board to the administrative structure.

ASSEMBLIES AND COURTS

The 1775 statute also allowed nobles and townspeople to hold assemblies at province and district levels. These assemblies met once every three years and had limited powers. Nobles had the right to elect marshals of the nobility, whose roles were to speak on their behalf to the local governor and central government and to head a group that cared for their widows and orphans. Townspeople elected town chiefs that had similar jobs.

Finally, the statute set up new law courts for each province. The highest courts were the criminal and the civil courts, in which members of all the estates were tried. Below them were separate courts for nobles, state peasants, and townspeople. Serfs were usually judged by their owners. Conscience, or equity, courts were also introduced. Anyone who had been under arrest without charge for over three days had the right to a hearing in a conscience court. There were so few of these courts, however, and they functioned so poorly, that they did little to help the legal system run well.

LOVE AND MARRIAGE

Throughout the political turmoil of the 1770s, Catherine still enjoyed a full private life. In 1772, she ended her relationship with Grigory Orlov. Two years later, she began a new affair with Guards officer Grigory Potemkin. Having lost an eye, Potemkin was not handsome, but he was brave, intelligent, funny, and the love of Catherine's life.

The life of Catherine's son Paul was also eventful during these years. His first wife, Natalya, died in April 1776, after a stillbirth. In September, he married another German princess, Sophia Dorothea of Württemberg, who took the name Maria Feodorovna. Soon, the couple produced two healthy boys, Alexander in 1777 and Constantine in 1779.

CHAPTER FIVE

HOME AND ABROAD

During the 1780s, Catherine the Great continued to be an extremely active ruler. At home in Russia, she introduced a wide range of major reforms. Abroad, she strove to enhance Russian power, both by acquiring territory and by acting as a mediator in international disputes.

IMPROVING EDUCATION

Peter the Great had worked hard to develop education in Russia. But by the time Catherine came to power, thousands of children were still not receiving adequate schooling—indeed many received none at all. Inspired by her Enlightenment beliefs, the empress thought that education could and should turn every child into "the ideal man and the perfect citizen." She set out to achieve this goal.

With the publication of the Statute for the Administration of the Provinces in 1775, Catherine introduced a systematic plan to improve education. The Statute required the Boards of Social Welfare to set up schools in all province and district towns. The empress continued her campaign in the 1780s. In 1782, she decided to introduce new, Austrian-style teaching methods and set up a Commission on National Schools to establish more schools, train more teachers, and provide more books. In 1786, she passed the Statute on National Schools.

In 1782, Catherine unveiled this statue of Peter the Great in St. Petersburg.

It introduced a new, two-tier school system for all children, except those of serfs.

THE CHARTER TO THE NOBLES

Catherine was also eager to extend the administrative and social reforms that she had begun during the previous decade. On April 21, 1785, she introduced two charters that legally defined and organized the estates of the nobility and the townspeople. In this way, she hoped to tie them more closely to the state, and so to herself as the empress.

The Charter to the Nobles listed the many rights, old and new, of the Russian nobility. These included immunity from corporal punishment and personal taxation, as well as the right to refuse state service and to own serfs. The charter also outlined how nobles were to participate in local government. Finally, it divided the nobles into six groups, according to how they had obtained noble status.

THE CHARTER TO THE TOWNS

The Charter to the Towns followed the pattern of the Charter to the Nobles by listing townspeople's rights as well as introducing major reforms. It divided townspeople, like nobles, into six groups. These included "eminent citizens"—people who had distinguished themselves in a particular role or were worth over 50,000 rubles —as well as merchants and craftworkers. It also set up two new local government institutions for each town. The town *duma,* or council, contained elected members from all six of the

In 1764, Catherine set up the Smolny
Institute, a school for noble girls in
St. Petersburg. A new school (above)
opened on its site in the 19th century.

Peasants who worked the land collected
hay from the fields to feed their animals.

groups of townspeople. It elected an execu-
tive council with six members—one from
each group—that effectively ran the town.

INDUSTRY AND TRADE

The great majority of people in 18th-century
Russia farmed the land to make a living. Peter
the Great, however, had encouraged the
development of industries, in particular the
mining of metals, the manufacture of
weapons, and the production of cloth.
Catherine believed agriculture would always
be more important than industry, but she still
tackled the problems of Russian industry
with her usual energy.

Most industrial workers were serfs or
assigned peasants who had been forced into
factories and mines because of labor short-
ages, and who were little more than serfs
themselves. The empress hoped to promote
the greater use of free labor, which she
believed was much more efficient. The
nobles, however, wanted to continue using

serf labor and to keep their exclusive rights to it. They managed to prevent the merchants and other non-nobles from owning serfs.

INDUSTRY AND THE STATE

Another major goal of Catherine's economic policy was to free industry from unnecessary state interference. In a 1775 manifesto, she had given people of all estates the right to set up any industry, anywhere in Russia. Most people, of course, did not have the money to take advantage of this new situation. A few, however, including some serfs, had become very wealthy industrialists. In the late 1770s, when it was no longer necessary to raise money for fighting the First Turkish War, the empress also abolished a wide range of industrial taxes.

Catherine's aims did not change during the 1780s. In 1782, she returned full control of their land to the nobility. Previously, the state had held some rights over crops grown in the soil and minerals found beneath it. This prompted more nobles to set up industries. In 1783, the empress allowed private individuals to set up printing presses, leading to a huge rise in the number of paper mills. Heavy industry thrived, as well. By 1800, Russia produced more pig iron than any other country.

Catherine collected fine art and also loved china pieces like these 18th-century items from St. Petersburg's Imperial Porcelain factory.

TRADE AND TARIFFS

The steady growth in industry prompted a far sharper growth in trade, both inside Russia and with other nations. Another major factor in this development was the gradual reduction in tariffs, or import taxes, organized by Catherine and her government. Tariffs reached their lowest in 1782, when the tariff on imported raw materials was two percent.

FOREIGN POLICY

The 1774 Treaty of Kutchuk Kainardji between Russia and the Ottoman Empire created only an uneasy peace. The Turks were determined to regain the land they had lost, while Catherine was eager to seize still more territory. By 1780, she had formulated the Greek Project, an ambitious plan to overthrow the Muslim Ottomans and recreate the Christian Byzantine Empire. She intended her grandson Constantine to rule this empire from Constantinople—the city that was once the Byzantine capital but was now the capital of the Ottoman Empire.

Catherine needed an ally to achieve her goal. Prussia, with which she already had a formal alliance, was the obvious choice. Frederick II, Prussia's ruler, however, wanted to avoid Russian encroachment into Europe, so he was unlikely to welcome the Greek Project. Catherine turned to Joseph II of Austria for help.

Joseph II shared Prussia's concerns about Russian expansion, but he had stronger reason to fear the Turks. Their presence to the south was a threat and had led to wars in the past. In 1780, he went to Russia for talks with Catherine. In 1781, the two signed a secret deal, each agreeing to support the other in case of Turkish attack or failure to abide by the Kutchuk Kainardji treaty.

The meeting between Catherine and Joseph II of Austria in 1780.

THE CRIMEA

Catherine made her first land gain of the 1780s without declaring war. Since 1774, her former lover, Grigory Potemkin, had been governor of Russia's most southerly provinces. The Treaty of Kutchuk Kainardji had made the neighboring Crimea independent, but both Russia and Turkey still sought to influence the region. In 1776, Russia invaded, and in July 1783, Catherine settled the question once and for all by ordering Potemkin to annex the territory. The Turks did not resist.

Russia's influence in the south, close to the Turkish border, now gradually increased. Georgia, a kingdom in the Caucasus region, was made a Russian protectorate in 1783. Then, in 1785, Russia set up a naval base in Sevastopol on the Crimea's southern tip. It directly faced the Ottomans across the Black Sea. In 1787, Catherine and Joseph II made a state visit to the Crimea, now also governed by Potemkin. He showed them only so-called "Potemkin villages," which had been specially cleaned up for the occasion.

A TURKISH ULTIMATUM

Since 1774, the Turks had suffered many affronts to their power—the loss of the Crimea, Russia's open intervention in Georgia, Russia's "secret" attempts to encourage revolt in Turkish-ruled territories, and more. Catherine's trip to the Crimea, during which she publicly reviewed Sevastopol's naval base, fuelled the Turks' anger further. The presence of another hostile European leader, Joseph II, only added to their fears.

The Turks presented Catherine's government with an ultimatum in July 1787. Among its demands were Russia's withdrawal from and abandonment of claims to Georgia, permission for Turks to search Russian ships in Turkish waters, and acceptance of Turkish consuls, or diplomatic representatives, in Russia and the Crimea. When they had received no reply by August, the Turks demanded the return of the Crimea. Their terms were turned down, so on August 24, 1787, they declared war on Russia.

THE SECOND TURKISH WAR

The war did not go well for Russia at first. Potemkin, the commander-in-chief of Russia's forces, suffered a failure of nerve during early battles for the Crimea and almost gave up. Meanwhile, Prussia and England declared their support for Turkey. There was good news in October 1787, when General Alexander Suvorov drove the Turks back from Kinburn, a Russian fort on the edge of the Crimea. Then, in February 1788, Emperor

This map shows the territories of the Russian and Ottoman Empires, as well as the major sites of the First and Second Turkish Wars.

RUSSIA AND THE AMERICAN REVOLUTION

In 1775, the inhabitants of Britain's thirteen North American colonies, inspired in part by the ideals of the Enlightenment, began a war to win their independence. At first, British king George III and his government asked Russia for help. Catherine, however, turned down their request for 20,000 troops, preferring instead to remain neutral. France, by contrast, joined in the conflict in 1778. As Britain's long-time enemy in both North America and Europe, France was more than content to take the side of the rebellious Americans.

In an effort to prevent weapons and other goods from reaching its enemies, Britain soon began to seize cargoes that ships from neutral nations were carrying to hostile ports in France and elsewhere. Russia objected, and in 1780, it encouraged other neutral countries, including Denmark, Sweden, and the Netherlands, to form the League of Armed Neutrality. The League's members armed their ships so they could defend their right to enter ports engaged in the war. It's efforts contributed to the eventual victory of the colonies over Britain in 1783.

Joseph II officially took Austria into the war on the Russian side.

Trouble, however, came from a different quarter. Sweden, Russia's old enemy to the north, had long wanted to regain land lost to Peter the Great. Gustavus III, Sweden's king, also wanted to punish Russia for supporting Swedish nobles who opposed his rule. In summer 1788, when many Russian troops were engaged in the south, he declared war on Russia. Soon his army and navy were on their way to St. Petersburg. Now the Russians had to fight on two fronts at the same time.

Meanwhile, in the south, the struggle centered on the Turkish fort of Ochakov, which fell to the Russians in December 1788. During the following year, the Russians slowly advanced into Turkish territory, eventually reaching the Dniester River. Further south, the Austrians captured Bucharest. Catherine was delighted with the progress of the troops, but she was also distracted by the news that, in mid-July, a violent revolution had broken out in France.

THE TREATY OF JASSY

The situation changed dramatically after Joseph II died in February 1790. In July, the new emperor of Austria, Leopold, signed a peace treaty with Turkey, leaving the Russians to fight alone. Happily for Catherine, the Swedish conflict ended a month later with the Treaty of Verela. Russia lost no land but had to accept the new form of government Gustavus III had established in Sweden. In December 1790, Russian forces took the Turkish fort of Izmail, and in June 1791, defeated the Turks at the Battle of Machin, south of the Danube River.

Following these setbacks, the Turks agreed to discuss peace terms, and in December 1791, signed the Treaty of Jassy. It confirmed Russia's annexation of the Crimea and gave the country more land on the Black Sea coast. These were important gains, but they did not meet the goals of the Greek Project.

LOVE AND LOSS

In the 1780s, Catherine had taken several new lovers, including Alexander Lanskoi and Platon Zubov. But these immature younger men—Catherine had turned 60 in 1789—never replaced Potemkin in her affections. In October 1791, after catching a fever at the Jassy peace talks, Potemkin died. When she heard the news, Catherine wrote, "A terrible bludgeon-stroke has just fallen on my head."

CHAPTER SIX

THE FINAL YEARS

Catherine's final years were clouded by both personal unhappiness and political uncertainty. As her health declined and her problems increased, the empress struggled to cope with the fast-changing world around her.

THE PROBLEM OF POLAND

At the end of the Second Turkish War, Stanislaus Poniatowski was still King of Poland. But since the First Partition of the country in 1772, anti-Russian feeling there had greatly increased. In 1790, Prussia made a formal alliance with Poland, promising to defend Poland from outside—in other words, Russian—interference. Then, in 1791, the Poles adopted a new constitution that made the monarchy hereditary, established a different form of government, and gave more rights to the middle classes and peasants.

This map shows the three partitions of Poland, which took place in 1772, 1793, and 1795.

Russia was not able to intervene in these events because it was busy with a bloody war against the Turks. After the war with the Turks was over, however, Catherine was determined to punish the Poles for their actions. Her resolve was increased by the fear that revolutionary fervor had spread to Poland from France and that without decisive action, it might infect Russia itself. In addition, the empress feared that a reborn Poland might be able to shake off Russian influence forever.

THE SECOND AND THIRD PARTITIONS

Before sending troops to Poland, Catherine informed Austria and Prussia of her plans. Austria protested, but Prussia—Poland's sworn defender—offered no opposition. On the contrary, Frederick William II, Prussia's king from 1786, welcomed the Russian invasion, hoping it might lead to territorial gains for his country. The invasion finally took place in May 1792. Without support from

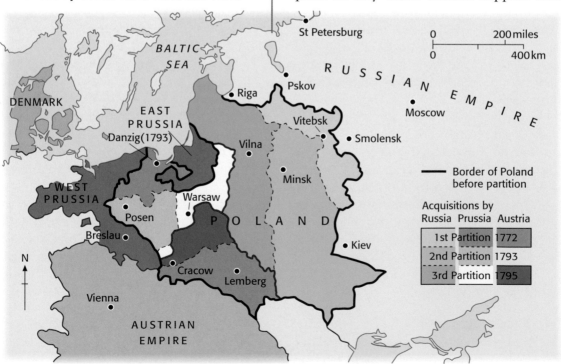

Prussia, Polish resistance collapsed, and a revised constitution was introduced.

Poland then suffered the Second Partition, which was completed in 1793. This time only Russia and Prussia took slices of its land: Russia gained almost 88,800 square miles (230,000 square kilometers) in the east, Prussia a smaller area in the west, along with the Baltic Sea port of Danzig. In 1794, the Poles mounted another revolt, which was

This cartoon from 1795 shows Russia, Prussia, and Austria dividing up Poland. Catherine the Great is seated on the left.

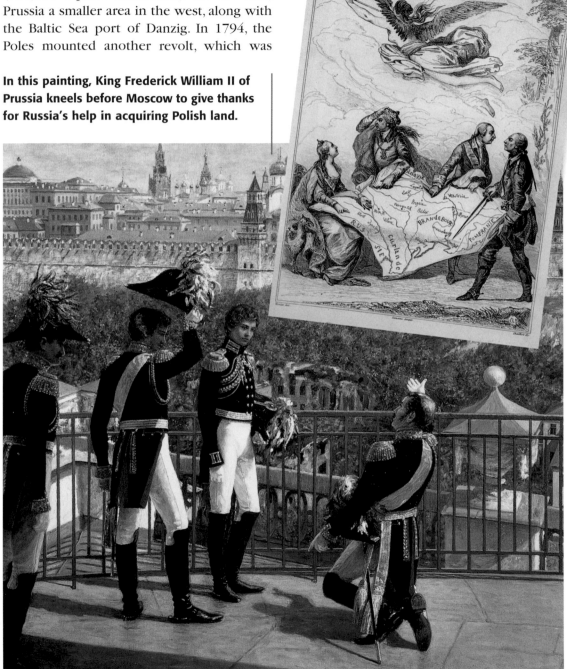

In this painting, King Frederick William II of Prussia kneels before Moscow to give thanks for Russia's help in acquiring Polish land.

The French Revolution began on July 14, 1789, when an angry mob attacked the Bastille, a prison in Paris.

quickly suppressed by Russian and Prussian troops. In 1795, the Third Partition divided the rest of Poland between Russia, Prussia, and Austria, and the country ceased to exist.

FEAR OF FRANCE

The French Revolution began in 1789, and it eventually removed French king Louis XVI from his throne. This event filled Catherine the Great with fear and loathing. She believed that a threat to one European monarch was a threat to all and that the "French madness" should not be allowed to spread. At this time, her Enlightenment belief in equality faded into the background, and a steely determination to preserve Russian autocracy came to the fore.

In 1792, France declared war on Austria and Prussia, who united to prevent the advance of French armies across Europe. In 1793, the year that King Louis XVI and his wife Marie Antoinette were finally executed, Britain joined in the fight against France. Although she strongly supported the actions of these anti-French powers, Catherine sent no troops to help them. Instead, she concentrated on tackling what she believed to be dangerous revolutionary activity at home.

CENSORSHIP AND SUPPRESSION

Within Russia, Catherine began trying to suppress all criticism of her rule, censoring publications—even the works of Voltaire—and punishing people she thought guilty of stirring up opposition to her.

Among the empress's first targets was a nobleman's son, Alexander Radishchev, who in 1790 published a book called *A Journey from St. Petersburg to Moscow*. In this book, Radishchev was openly critical of autocratic government—though not of Catherine herself—as well as of the corruption, inefficiency, and brutality of local officials. In addition, it described the terrible conditions endured by serfs and suggested that they should be gradually emancipated. For his honesty and concern, Radishchev was sentenced to 10 years in exile in Siberia's Ilimski fort.

Publisher Nikolai Novikov was another victim of Catherine's antirevolutionary zeal. He produced a range of journals, many of which described the same problems and abuses of power as Radishchev's book. Some also explained the beliefs of the Freemasons, a group to which Novikov belonged. Catherine distrusted Freemasonry, which she considered to be a cover for revolutionary activity. In 1792, the publisher was sentenced, without trial, to 15 years in prison.

DEATH OF AN EMPRESS

Despite her concentration on problems at home, Catherine played a small part in preventing the French advance across Europe. Beginning in 1793, she provided Britain with ships to help block deliveries to French ports. In 1796, after the French general Napoleon Bonaparte had inflicted several defeats on the Austrians in northern Italy, Catherine began preparing to send about 60,000 troops to the Austrians' aid. But by that time, the 67-year-old empress, overweight and plagued by rheumatism, was far from well.

The end came in St. Petersburg's Winter Palace, late in 1796. On November 5, Catherine suffered a stroke that left her paralyzed and unconscious. Despite his best efforts, Dr. Rogerson, her physician from Scotland, was unable to revive her. The empress died the following day with Platon Zubov at her bedside. There had been a possibility that Alexander, Catherine's oldest grandchild, would inherit the throne, but this came to nothing. Catherine's son Paul, who matched her neither in humanity nor intellect, prepared to rule the Russian Empire.

CATHERINE AND THE JEWS

An *ukaz* issued by Catherine the Great in 1773 declared: "As Almighty God tolerated on earth all faiths, tongues and creeds, so Her Majesty, starting from the same principles, and in accordance with His Holy Will, proposed to follow in the same path." In fact, the empress followed a policy of religious toleration from early in her reign, allowing most of her subjects to practice their chosen faiths as long as it did not interfere with their duties to the state. During the 1760s, she also permitted the limited resettlement of Jews in Russia. Earlier intolerance and anti-Semitism had led to the official expulsion of the Jews in 1727.

As Catherine's reign progressed, both Jewish settlers and Polish Jews who found themselves living in Russia after the 1772 First Partition became increasingly integrated into Russian life. Some were elected as local government officials, and in 1786, all were granted legal equality with non-Jews. They were, however, still expected to live in designated areas and still faced anti-Semitism from the rest of Russia's population. The Jews' situation changed again in 1794, a year after the Second Partition brought more Jews into Russia. From then on, they were taxed double the amount paid by Christians.

ENLIGHTENMENT EMPRESS OR OLD-FASHIONED AUTOCRAT?

Catherine the Great was a devoted follower of the intellectual movement known as the Enlightenment, and she openly praised its ideals of reason, progress, and reform. Nonetheless, she made only limited changes to traditional Russian society and reigned as an absolute ruler, just as her predecessors had done. Was she an Enlightenment empress, an old-fashioned autocrat, or a little of both? Read both sides of the argument and the sources, then judge for yourself.

ENLIGHTENMENT EMPRESS?

SOURCE 1

He [Count Gyllenburg, the Swedish envoy to the Russian court] *had always maintained in Hamburg that I had a philosophical turn of mind and asked what was happening to my philosophy in the whirlwind in which I was now living. I told him of the hours I spent in my room, reading. He said that a fifteen-year-old philosopher was too young yet for self-knowledge and . . . that I should nourish* [my spirit] *with the best possible reading and to this effect recommended to me . . . the* Causes of Greatness and Decadence of the Roman Republic *by Montesquieu.*
(FROM *THE MEMOIRS OF CATHERINE THE GREAT*)

SOURCE 2

The king is worthy of kingship only if he forgets himself and sacrifices himself for the common good. . . . Absolute power in a king ends with him having precisely as many slaves as he has subjects.
(FROM *TÉLÉMAQUE*, BY FRANÇOIS FÉNELON)

ENLIGHTENMENT IDEALS

Catherine's interest in Enlightenment ideals began before she became empress in 1762. Her memoirs show that she was a serious reader from a young age (*Source 1*) and followed an intense program of self-education. This included studying works by Enlightenment thinkers such as Charles de Montesquieu, Voltaire, and François Fénelon (*Source 2*). Notes that she wrote to herself prove her ideals were sincere (*Source 3*).

A bust of Catherine II.

CATHERINE AND DIDEROT

Once she came to power, Catherine began to build friendships with great Enlightenment thinkers. Nine days after her accession, she invited French intellectual Denis Diderot to Russia. She wanted him to continue to work while in Russia on the *Encyclopédie* (right), a multivolume encyclopedia of the Enlightenment. Diderot refused, but he visited Russia from 1773 to 1774.

CATHERINE AND VOLTAIRE

Catherine's closest philosophical friendship, however, was with Voltaire. The two exchanged letters from 1763 to 1777, allowing Catherine to learn about the Frenchman's ideas and to consult him about her plans. Early in her reign, she asked him to comment on the *Bolshoi Nakaz*. As usual, he responded with great flattery.

THE BOLSHOI NAKAZ

The *Bolshoi Nakaz*, which Catherine produced in 1767, is proof of her commitment to Enlightenment ideals. It demonstrated that her beliefs were not simply for discussion with like-minded people but for guiding the Legislative Commission and shaping the future of Russia. The paragraphs of the *Nakaz* (*Source 4*) make the empress's aims clear. She was not to blame that the Commission achieved almost nothing.

RUSSIA'S REFORMS

Despite the Commission's failure, Catherine pressed on with her plans. Her reforms of local government, law, welfare, and education were all inspired by Enlightenment ideals. Parts of the 1775 Statute for the Administration of the Provinces and the 1785 Charters to the Nobles and the Towns, for example, were directly influenced by Montesquieu's *Spirit of the Laws*. This work stated that society should be composed of clearly defined estates and that administrative and judicial powers should be separated.

A plate from the Encyclopédie showing instrument-makers at work.

INTELLECTUAL ACHIEVEMENT

True to her Enlightenment belief in learning, Catherine also promoted intellectual and cultural achievement. She patronized architects, built a theater in the Winter Palace, and, in 1783, established the Russian Academy of Letters. The Russian Academy of Letters produced the first Russian dictionary 11 years later. The empress also supported many writers, and she wrote a great deal herself, including articles in the periodical *All Sorts of Things* (1769).

ENLIGHTENMENT EMPRESS

Throughout her reign, Catherine the Great remained faithful to the Enlightenment ideals that inspired most of her policy-making. Her inability to follow them through completely was caused not by her own failings, but by her subjects' resistance to new ideas (*Source 5*).

SOURCE 3

Be gentle, humane, accessible, compassionate, and liberal-minded: do not let your grandeur prevent you from condescending with kindness toward the small and putting yourselves in their place. See that this kindness, however, does not weaken your authority, nor diminish their respect. Listen to anything which seems to deserve attention.
(NOTE BY CATHERINE FOUND IN HER COPY OF *TÉLÉMAQUE*)

SOURCE 4

*33. The Laws ought to be so framed, as to secure the Safety of every Citizen as much as possible.
34. The Equality of all Citizens consists in this; that they should all be subject to the same Laws.
35. This Equality requires Institutions so well adapted, as to prevent the Rich from oppressing those who are not so wealthy as themselves. . . .*
(PARAGRAPHS FROM THE *BOLSHOI NAKAZ*)

SOURCE 5

You work on paper, which will suffer anything. As for me, poor empress, I work on human skin, which is quite otherwise; irritable and ticklish.
(EXTRACT FROM A CONVERSATION BETWEEN CATHERINE AND DIDEROT DURING HIS VISIT TO RUSSIA)

ENLIGHTENMENT EMPRESS OR OLD-FASHIONED AUTOCRAT?

OLD-FASHIONED AUTOCRAT?

SOURCE 6

9. The Sovereign is absolute; for there is no other Authority but that which centres in his single Person, that can act with a Vigour proportionate to the extent of such a vast Dominion [Russia].
10. The Extent of the Dominion requires an absolute Power to be vested in that Person who rules over it. . . .
(PARAGRAPHS FROM THE BOLSHOI NAKAZ)

SOURCE 7

If there existed someone extravagant enough to say: you believe that the grandeur of the Russian Empire demands an autocratic ruler, but I set no value on this grandeur, so long as every citizen lives happily – I would reply to this madman: you should know that if your government became a republic, it would lose all its power and the land would become the prey of anyone who cared to seize it.
(EXTRACT FROM CATHERINE'S PRIVATE PAPERS)

SOURCE 8

. . . the Empress of Russia is certainly a despot, since, whatever the true end of her government, it makes all liberty and property depend on one person.
(DENIS DIDEROT)

AN AUTOCRATIC RULER

Catherine the Great's genuine interest in Enlightenment thought cannot be denied—her writings provide the proof. In this interest, she was only following the fashion among rulers of the time. Frederick II of Prussia and Joseph II of Austria, for example, also admired Enlightenment thinkers. There is no evidence, however, that the empress wished to follow Enlightenment principles that would require reordering Russian society completely. Both the *Bolshoi Nakaz* and her private papers (*Sources 6* and *7, respectively*) show that Catherine believed autocracy would always be right for Russia.

PHILOSOPHICAL FRIENDSHIPS

The Enlightenment philosophers that Catherine befriended were not all as uncritical of her as Voltaire. To Diderot, it was clear that Catherine's Enlightenment principles were limited and would never involve sharing power (*Source 8*). On his visit to Russia, he clashed with Catherine several times. Back in France, he wrote *Observations on Her Imperial Majesty's Instructions to the Deputies on the Making of Laws*. It was not compli-mentary and Catherine was furious (*Source 9*).

Denis Diderot

REPRESSING REBELLION

As Catherine's reign progressed, her ideals faded. The Pugachev Revolt filled her with rage. Although she acted mercifully in its immediate aftermath—many rebels were not punished—she

soon cracked down. More troops were stationed in the countryside, Cossacks were brought under control, and the 1785 Charter to the Nobles restated the privileges of Russia's highest estate. Talk of serfs' rights ceased, and the state and the nobility united to keep the serfs firmly in their place.

ENLIGHTENED REFORMS?

The reforms Catherine introduced during the middle of her reign owed something to Enlightenment ideals, and local government and education were improved as a result. But it is important to remember that serfs, who made up more than half the population, were excluded from both local government bodies and schools and were allowed little access to courts. Catherine did absolutely nothing to right this wrong.

RESPONSE TO REVOLUTION

During the 1790s, the uproar in Poland and the horrors of the French Revolution caused Catherine to all but abandon her Enlightenment views. Her main goal now was to protect the Russian monarchy. Achieving this goal involved censorship and the imprisonment of any intellectuals who dared to question the way in which Russia was run. In 1793, after King Louis XVI was executed, Catherine broke off both diplomatic relations and trade with France (*Source 10*).

The execution of King Louis XVI, 1793.

OLD-FASHIONED AUTOCRAT

By her own admission, Catherine was essentially an old-fashioned autocrat, who nevertheless tried to use her power wisely (*Source 11*). She embraced the ideals of the Enlightenment when it suited her but—especially late in her reign—ignored them when it did not.

SOURCE 9

This piece [The Observations] is a real hotchpotch, without any common-sense, judgment or insight. If my Instructions [the Nakaz] had been to Diderot's taste, everything would have been turned upside down.
(CATHERINE IN A LETTER TO BARON FRIEDRICH GRIMM, A FRIEND)

SOURCE 10

We consider it our duty before God and our own conscience not to tolerate any further relations between our empire and France such as normally exist between well-ordered states, until the justice of the Most High [God] punishes the malefactors [wrong-doers], and it pleases His holy will to put an end to the misfortunes of that kingdom, returning it to order and the forces of legitimate rule.
(EXTRACT FROM AN *UKAZ* ISSUED BY CATHERINE IN 1789)

SOURCE 11

In the first place my orders would not be carried out unless they were the kind of orders which could be carried out; you know with what prudence and circumspection I act in the promulgation [passing] of my laws. I examine the circumstances, I take advice, I consult. . . . And when I am already convinced in advance of general approval, then I issue my orders, and have the pleasure of observing what you call blind obedience. And that is the foundation of unlimited power.
(CATHERINE TO VASILY POPOV, ONE OF POTEMKIN'S OFFICIALS)

THE SERFS' FRIEND OR THE SERFS' ENEMY?

Serfs were the largest class of people in Catherine the Great's Russia. By the end of her reign, the number of serfs had reached more than 5.6 million, making up about 54 percent of the country's population. Before she came to the throne, the empress had made plans to help these men and women, the poorest of Russia's poor. But was she true to them, or did she abandon the serfs to support the nobles? Read both sides of the argument and the sources, then judge for yourself.

THE SERFS' FRIEND?

SOURCE 1

*. . . two boys for sale, one 17 and the other 14 years old, both good behaviour, the latter trained as a barber. Their price 500 roubles.
. . . for sale a man of good behaviour, who is trained in millinery and who can be used as a yardman and coachman. Also for sale an almost new carriage wheel.*
(EXTRACTS FROM THE *ST. PETERSBURG GAZETTE*)

SOURCE 2

It is against Christian religion and justice to make slaves out of men, born to be free. All peasants who were formerly slaves are freed by a council, in Germany, France, Spain, etc. To carry out such a revolution would not make one popular with land-owners. But here is an easy solution; to make a rule from now on for anyone selling land, that at the moment the new owner takes possession, all serfs are declared free. In about a hundred years . . . we should have a free nation.
(EXTRACT FROM A NOTE MADE BY CATHERINE)

SERF LIFE

Russian serfs had few rights. They had to pay their noble owners *obrok* (fees for use of the land) and perform *barshchina* (compulsory labor). They were not allowed to own land or a house. They could not move—and sometimes could not even marry—without their owners' consent. Often, serfs had to obey special legal codes their owners had devised. Many serfs, especially those who worked in nobles' homes, were bought and sold (*Source 1*).

CATHERINE'S CONCERN

Catherine began to consider the issue of the serfs before she came to the throne. In a note from about 1761, she outlined a plan to end serfdom (*Source 2*). Once in power, Catherine asked officials to find ways of tackling the problem. One idea was to grant serfs land leases that gave them legal rights.

Serfs at work threshing grain.

THE *BOLSHOI NAKAZ*

Catherine dealt with the question of serfdom in Chapter XI of the *Bolshoi Nakaz*, and its paragraphs make her views clear (*Source 3*). In fact, the empress's first draft of the *Nakaz* spoke out against serfdom even more forcefully. In the final version, however, she toned down her comments, probably to avoid upsetting the nobles.

THE LEGISLATIVE COMMISSION

There were lengthy debates on the status of serfs during the meetings of the Legislative Commission, although no serfs, of course, were present. A few nobles, including a man named Korobin, who may have been Catherine's secret spokesman, attacked the institution of serfdom. But in general, the nobility resisted change, to the empress's great disgust (*Source 4*).

A serf couple and their child bow before their noble owner.

LATER DEVELOPMENTS

After the collapse of the Legislative Commission, Catherine realized that most nobles would never willingly give up their right to own serfs. As a result, she began trying to help these peasants in other ways. In 1771, she made public serf auctions illegal, and in 1775, she banned the enserfment of free men and women. The same document decreed that only hereditary nobles could own serfs. Also in 1775, she ordered officials to stop nobles from mistreating their serfs.

THE SERFS' FRIEND

Catherine was always committed to helping the serfs. But in this, as in so many fields of policy-making, she was hindered not just by the nobles, but by the reality of life in 18th-century Russia (*Source 5*). Still, she did as much as she could under the circumstances and was genuinely the serfs' friend.

SOURCE 3

*252. . . . as the Law of Nature commands us to take as much Care, as lies in our power, of the Prosperity of all the People; we are obliged to alleviate the Situation of the Subjects, as much as sound Reason will permit.
253. And therefore, to shun all Occasions of reducing People to a State of Slavery, except the utmost Necessity should inevitably oblige us to do it; in that Case, it ought not to be done for our own benefit; but for the State. . . .*
(PARAGRAPHS FROM THE *BOLSHOI NAKAZ*)

SOURCE 4

What had I not to suffer from. . . . irrational and cruel public opinion when this question was considered in the Legislative Commission. The mob of nobles began to suspect that these discussions might bring about an improvement in the position of the peasants. . . . I believe that there were not twenty human beings who reflected on the subject at that time with humanity. . . .
(EXTRACT FROM CATHERINE'S WRITINGS)

SOURCE 5

. . . where Catherine could narrow down the range of those entitled to own serfs, reduce the ways by which people were enserfed, and increase the security of those who had been freed, she did so.
(EXTRACT FROM *RUSSIA IN THE AGE OF CATHERINE THE GREAT*, BY ISABEL DE MADARIAGA)

THE SERFS' FRIEND OR THE SERFS' ENEMY?

THE SERFS' ENEMY?

SOURCE 6

Because the well-being of a state, in accordance with the Laws of God and all the laws of the people, requires that all and everyone shall remain upon his estate and shall be assured of his rights, we decide to preserve to the landowners the right to their estates and properties, and to keep the peasants in necessary obedience to them.
(EXTRACT FROM A DECREE ISSUED BY CATHERINE IN JULY 1762)

SOURCE 7

Nobles did not have the right to execute a serf, but they could choose a punishment which would almost certainly result in death. Hundreds, or even thousands of blows could be inflicted, leading to the maiming or death of serfs; other nobles kept instruments for punishment, including spiked collars and stocks [a wooden frame with holes in which the head and hands were locked]. Houseserfs were particularly vulnerable to the whims and tempers of their masters, and often their mistresses. One noblewoman is said to have whipped 80 female houseserfs for not collecting wild strawberries when she asked.
(EXTRACT FROM A SOCIAL HISTORY OF THE RUSSIAN EMPIRE 1650-1825, BY JANET M. HARTLEY)

EARLY YEARS

Catherine the Great often wrote and spoke in favor of the serfs. But even early in her reign, it was clear that her support for them was limited. Just a week after she came to power, the empress issued an *ukaz*, or decree, telling landowners that their right to keep serfs would continue (*Source 6*).

Flogging a serf with a knout, a type of whip.

REASONS FOR REVOLT

Unrest among serfs increased after Catherine's accession. A major cause of this was her failure to overturn Peter III's 1762 decree that ended compulsory state service by the nobility. Serfs saw no reason why they should be obliged to serve nobles when the nobles now had no obligations. The empress sent troops to end the revolts and then made serfs pay for them.

PUNISHMENT AND PROHIBITION

Catherine also introduced new measures that harmed serfs. In 1765, she gave owners the right to send disobedient serfs to the navy for hard labor. In 1767, she restated a ban on serfs complaining directly to Russia's ruler about their masters. Complaints had grown common. Under Catherine, complainers were regularly punished by flogging or exile.

MINOR MEASURES

The measures Catherine introduced to help serfs during the 1770s were minor and, in any case, were not enforced. Serf auctions continued. While only about six landowners were

46

punished for mistreating their serfs during her reign, harsh punishments for serfs who broke owners' private legal codes remained common (*Source 7*).

PUGACHEV AND AFTER

Serfs were so far from seeing Catherine as their friend that thousands of them supported the 1773–1774 Pugachev Revolt. After the revolt was over, the empress did little to address the grievances Pugachev had expressed. Instead, she tried to bring serfs under tighter control and to make people forget the revolt—for example, by destroying Pugachev's house.

SUPPRESSING OPPOSITION

As her reign continued, Catherine acted to confirm the nobility's power over the serfs, especially in the 1785 Charter to the Nobles. After the French Revolution broke out in 1789, she began to punish anyone—for example, writer Alexander Radishchev— who dared to speak out on the serfs' behalf (*Sources 8 and 9*).

INCREASING NUMBERS

Catherine did not manage even to reduce the number of serfs in Russia. By the end of her reign, there were more serfs than there were when she took power (*Source 10*). Among the new serfs were about 60,000 former court peasants given by Catherine to her supporters. She also created about 340,000 serfs in the Polish and other non-Russian lands she annexed.

Alexander Radishchev

THE SERFS' ENEMY

Catherine's desire to improve serfs' lives was always superficial. She supported the nobles from early in her reign and steadily increased their power. She also helped serf numbers to grow, and she eventually blocked attempts at social change. She can honestly be called the serfs' enemy.

SOURCE 8

The agriculturists [serfs] *are even to this day slaves among us; we do not recognize them as fellow citizens equal to ourselves, and we have forgotten that they are men. O beloved fellow citizens! O true sons of the fatherland! Look about you and see the error of your ways!*

(EXTRACT FROM *A JOURNEY FROM ST. PETERSBURG TO MOSCOW*, BY ALEXANDER RADISHCHEV)

SOURCE 9

The purpose of this book is clear on every page: its author, infected and full of the French madness [the ideals of the French Revolution], *is trying in every possible way to break down respect for authority and for the authorities, to stir up in the people indignation against their superiors and the government.*

(EXTRACT FROM CATHERINE'S NOTES ON RADISHCHEV'S BOOK)

SOURCE 10

YEAR	NUMBER OF MALE SERFS IN RUSSIA*	PERCENTAGE OF RUSSIAN POPULATION
1762	4,422,021	55.47
1782	5,132,366	53.16
1795	5,686,223	54.47

* ACCURATE FIGURES ARE NOT AVAILABLE FOR FEMALE SERFS

EDUCATION POLICY—SUCCESS OR FAILURE?

In accordance with her Enlightenment ideals, Catherine the Great believed strongly in the importance of education. She read widely on the subject, studied the school systems of other countries, and set up commissions to consider the best way to improve education in Russia. Then, during the 1770s and 1780s, she introduced many educational reforms. But did they benefit Russia's children, or did the empress's achievements fail to match up to her grand plans? Read both sides of the argument and the sources, then judge for yourself.

SUCCESS?

SOURCE 1

§1 . . . I think I may say that of all the men we meet with, nine parts of ten are what they are, good or evil, useful or not, by their education. 'Tis that which makes the great difference in mankind. . . .
§32 . . . If what I have said in the beginning of this discourse be true [see §1], as I do not doubt but it is . . . we have reason to conclude that great care is to be had of the forming children's minds and giving them that seasoning early which shall influence their lives always after. For when they do well or ill the praise or blame will be laid there. . . .
(EXTRACTS FROM *SOME THOUGHTS CONCERNING EDUCATION*, BY JOHN LOCKE)

SCHOOL SYSTEMS

A patchwork of schools operated in 18th-century Russia. Some primary education was provided by priests. Some landowners also held classes on their estates to teach peasants reading and writing. At the secondary level, there were grammar schools for priests' children, garrison schools for soldiers' children, and specialist schools, such as the Army Cadet Corps, for the military élite.

FIRST STEPS

Inspired by thinkers such as Englishman John Locke (*Source 1*), Catherine quickly set out to improve Russian education. Her first step, in 1764, was to set up a commission, but it achieved little. An important document, however, was published the same year. This was the *General Plan for the Education of Young People of both Sexes,* written by the empress's education adviser, Ivan Betskoi (*Source 2*). Catherine also set up two schools in 1764, a foundling home in Moscow and the Smolny Institute for Noble Girls in St. Petersburg, the first girls' school in Russia.

John Locke

THE *BOLSHOI NAKAZ* AND THE LEGISLATIVE COMMISSION

In the late 1760s, Catherine pressed on with her plan to introduce a nationwide system of schooling. She made her

commitment to education plain in the *Bolshoi Nakaz* of 1767 (*Source 3*) and ordered a subcommission of the Legislative Commission to examine the question proper education. It did so from 1768 to 1771, it but came to no conclusions.

THE STATUTE FOR THE ADMINISTRATION OF THE PROVINCES

Catherine's first major educational reform was introduced in 1775, as part of the Statute for the Administration of the Provinces. It set up Boards of Social Welfare and gave each board 15,000 rubles to establish schools and other institutions in every province and district town. The quality of the new schools, however, varied greatly from place to place.

Two pupils of the Smolny Institute.

THE COMMISSION ON NATIONAL SCHOOLS

Catherine decided the state should intervene more closely so that education could be standardized. In 1782, she founded the Commission on National Schools. Following the educational system used in Austria, the Commission set up new state schools and brought private schools into the state system. New teacher training colleges were also opened, and a range of new textbooks were published.

THE STATUTE ON NATIONAL SCHOOLS

Catherine's final educational reform was the 1786 Statute on National Schools (*Source 4*). It introduced free schooling for all children except those of serfs. There was to be a high and a primary school in the capital of each province and a primary school in the main town of each district. A new curriculum was set up, and corporal punishment was banned.

SCHOOL SUCCESS

During Catherine's reign, the education system of the past was replaced by a nationwide network of schools in which all pupils studied the same curriculum. Girls benefited especially, receiving the right to education for the first time.

SOURCE 2

The emphasis [of the General Plan] *was on the creation of a 'new kind of person', a new generation, which could only be achieved by isolating the child completely from the age of 5 to 21 from the harmful influences of parents and an illiterate, brutal and corrupt society. Schools were to stress not professional or vocational training but the creation of good citizens and accomplished human beings.*
(EXTRACT FROM *RUSSIA IN THE AGE OF CATHERINE THE GREAT,* BY ISABEL DE MADARIAGA)

SOURCE 3

248. Finally, the most sure, but, at the same *Time, the* most difficult *Expedient* [way] *to mend the Morals of the People, is a perfect System of Education.*
(EXTRACT FROM THE *BOLSHOI NAKAZ*)

SOURCE 4

Institutions are to be established in which young people will be taught in their native language on the basis of general prescriptions [rules]. *Such institutions must exist in all provinces and districts of the Russian empire under the name of national schools, which are divided into high schools and primary schools. In every provincial capital there must be one national high school consisting of four grades in which pupils will be taught . . . in their native tongue.*
(EXTRACT FROM THE STATUTE ON NATIONAL SCHOOLS, 1786)

EDUCATION POLICY—SUCCESS OR FAILURE?

FAILURE?

SOURCE 5

350. It is impossible to give a general Education to a very numerous People, and to bring up all the Children in Houses regulated for that Purpose. . . .
(EXTRACT FROM THE *BOLSHOI NAKAZ*)

SOURCE 6

Children must almost never be beaten, and the example of cruel punishments by mindless and savage schoolmasters must not be followed, since by such punishments, children are humiliated and lowered. . . . All forms of beating, apart from the pain, are, in accordance with all knowledge of all physical principles, harmful to health.
(EXTRACT FROM THE EXTENDED VERSION OF IVAN BETSKOI'S *GENERAL PLAN*, PUBLISHED IN 1766)

VISION AND REALITY

Catherine the Great's commitment to education was genuine. But there was a huge gulf between her vision of an educated country full of responsible citizens and the grim reality of 18th-century Russia. Even she acknowledged that her reforms could be only limited (*Source 5*).

EARLY SETBACKS

The schools set up early in Catherine's reign achieved far less than was hoped. The foundling homes in Moscow (1764) and St. Petersburg (1767) were intended as showcases for Ivan Betskoi's *General Plan*. In the event, so many children died— in 1764, 424 of the 523 babies at the Moscow home died— that teaching quality was irrelevant.

THE STATUTE FOR THE ADMINISTRATION OF THE PROVINCES

The educational good intentions of the Statute for the Administration of the Provinces (1775) soon went astray. It resulted in the foundation of a hodgepodge of schools, some public, some private. Nobles often refused to send their children to the same schools as townspeople, so money had to be found for two establishments in a town instead of one. State funds were short, so if local nobles would not contribute and the local governor was really not interested in schooling, little or nothing was achieved.

GROWING PROBLEMS

Catherine's reforms in the 1780s brought new problems. The Austrian-style schooling that she introduced forced all schools to be alike. An

An early Russian school. The teacher on the left is flogging one of his pupils.

adviser from Austria made sure every pupil learned the same lessons. Even successful private schools were closed. Often the Boards of Social Welfare which ran the new schools could not afford books and equipment. Teachers' salaries and morale were low. Many teachers taught while drunk and beat pupils, even though corporal punishment was banned (*Source 6*).

PUBLIC RESISTANCE

Parents often made matters worse. Those who sent boys to school often kept girls at home, believing their education to be unnecessary. As a result, the number of female pupils remained low (*Source 7*). Many townspeople saw no point in their children learning nonvocational subjects such as history, so they withdrew them from school early (*Source 8*). Many peasants never sent their children to school at all.

PUPIL NUMBERS

Statistics prove how limited Catherine's reforms were. By 1792, 302 national schools had been established, but they were attended by only 17,500 pupils. Historians estimate that, taking grammar and other types of school into account, the total number of pupils in Russia was about 62,000. At the time, the country's population was about 25 million.

Prussian monk Johann Ignaz Von Felbiger devised the principles on which Austrian, and later Russian, educational systems were based.

SCHOOL FAILURE

There were many flaws in Catherine's reforms. She established only a few hundred badly funded schools, many staffed by poor teachers. She set up no schools in rural areas and excluded all serf children from education. For these reasons and more (*Source 9*), her policy was an obvious failure.

SOURCE 7

YEAR	BOYS IN NATIONAL SCHOOLS	GIRLS IN NATIONAL SCHOOLS	PUPIL TOTAL
1782	474	44	518
1792	16,322	1,178	17,500

SOURCE 8

The numbers in the third and fourth classes were small. The second class pupils usually did not wish to go on to the third class, because the parents and the pupils themselves did not see the value in studying the higher classes. . . .
(EXTRACT FROM A REPORT BY NATIONAL SCHOOL INSPECTOR OSIP KOZODAVLEV)

SOURCE 9

The principal drawbacks to [education] expansion, as before, were Russia's inadequate financial resources and social prejudice among the privileged. Many nobles and merchants still saw schooling as a luxury, and of course serfs were automatically debarred from attending.
(EXTRACT FROM THE MAKING OF MODERN RUSSIA, BY LIONEL KOCHAN AND JOHN KEEP)

JUDGE
FOR YOURSELF

THE REFORM OF LOCAL GOVERNMENT—REALITY OR ILLUSION?

With the Statute for the Administration of the Provinces in 1775, Catherine the Great sought to transform Russia's ramshackle administrative, legal, and financial systems. But were the new institutions that she set up, often with great official ceremonies and celebrations, really any better than the old ones? Or were they made completely ineffective by corrupt, untrained personnel, just like those they replaced? Read both sides of the argument and the sources, then judge for yourself.

REALITY?

SOURCE 1

From the government's point of view, the success of Pugachev's motley forces could be ascribed to the 'weakness, laziness, negligence, idleness, disputes, disagreements, corruption and injustice' of local officials, and 'the weak conduct of both military and civil leaders.'
(EXTRACT FROM *RUSSIA IN THE AGE OF CATHERINE THE GREAT*, BY ISABEL DE MADARIAGA, CONTAINING QUOTATIONS FROM OFFICIAL RUSSIAN DOCUMENTS)

SOURCE 2

That the king can do no wrong is a necessary and fundamental principle of the English constitution. . . . It is better that ten guilty persons escape than one innocent suffer.
(EXTRACTS FROM *COMMENTARIES ON THE LAWS OF ENGLAND*, BY SIR WILLIAM BLACKSTONE)

Catherine the Great with a statue of the Goddess of Justice.

REASONS FOR REFORM

Eighteenth-century Russia was a brutal society. Violent conflicts regularly erupted and gangs of robbers were always on the prowl. The country's local government structures were inadequate to the task of controlling such lawlessness. Although Catherine the Great began to investigate this issue early in her reign, she introduced reforms only after the Pugachev Revolt made her realize the scale of the problem (*Source 1*).

CAREFUL PREPARATION

To ensure she acted wisely, Catherine read books such as *Commentaries on the Laws of England*, by William Blackstone, which gave her new ideas about legal systems (*Source 2*). She also consulted provincial governors, in particular, Jacob Sievers of Novgorod. Only then, in 1775, did she produce the Statute for the Administration of the Provinces.

THE STATUTE FOR THE ADMINISTRATION OF THE PROVINCES

The Statute set up complex new administrative and court systems. Equity courts were a major innovation, allowing judges to grant bail and take criminals' circumstances into account before sentencing. Officials called procurators were

52

also appointed for all courts. Their role was to check to see that laws were correctly applied and to report back to the General Procurator in St. Petersburg.

CRIME AND PUNISHMENT

The 1775 Statute made a Board of Social Welfare part of the administrative structure of each province. The Boards received money to establish not only schools and workhouses, but also houses of correction where lazy serfs and other criminals could be sent for punishment. Law enforcement was strengthened by the Police Code of 1782, which set up Police Boards, increased the number of police, and broadened their duties (*Source 3*).

MEASURING SUCCESS

During a trip that Catherine made through five provinces in 1780, inspectors reported that many administrative bodies had already been set up (*Source 4*) and that the new courts were working quickly. This was still true in 1786, when St. Petersburg courts dealt with an amazing 52,427 cases. The number of officials grew quickly after 1775 (*Source 5*), improving administrative performance.

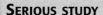

English judge and law professor Sir William Blackstone.

SERIOUS STUDY

Catherine did not require officials to study law or any other subject relevant to their posts. Documents left by a few officials, however, show that some did so voluntarily, spending six months or more acquiring legal knowledge. The empress encouraged a professional attitude to legal work by funding Moscow University's first law professorship in 1773.

REAL REFORMS

Catherine the Great established a comprehensive new legal and administrative framework for Russia. As a result, the country was better run, and justice was quicker and easier to obtain. The increase in the number of local officials and police added to the general improvement.

SOURCE 3

They [the police] *could deal summarily with petty crime, such as thefts of under 20 roubles (too petty to be worthy of the attention of the courts) and minor problems of disorder, such as begging and drunkenness. . . . At the same time . . . the police were given ambitious and wide-ranging responsibilities for the maintenance of buildings, paving of streets, prevention of fires, sanitation and erection of lamp-posts.*
(EXTRACT FROM *A SOCIAL HISTORY OF THE RUSSIAN EMPIRE 1650-1825*, BY JANET M. HARTLEY)

SOURCE 4

Governments established according to the new pattern	29
Towns constructed	144
Treaties concluded	30
Victories	78
Memorable edicts and laws	88
Edicts for improving the life of the people	138
	492

(A LIST OF HER GREATEST ACHIEVEMENTS PRESENTED TO CATHERINE BY PRINCE BEZBORODKO, ONE OF HER SECRETARIES, IN 1781. THE REFORM OF LOCAL GOVERNMENT AND THE RELATED CONSTRUCTION OF TOWNS APPEARS AT THE TOP.)

SOURCE 5

YEAR	NUMBER OF LOCAL GOVERNMENT OFFICIALS
1774	12,712
1781	22,000
1796	27,000

JUDGE
FOR YOURSELF

THE REFORM OF LOCAL GOVERNMENT—REALITY OR ILLUSION?

ILLUSION?

NOBLE AIMS

Catherine's aims in the field of local government were noble. She truly intended to make her country run more smoothly. However, she was thwarted by circumstance and by the failure of her subjects to share her high ideals.

APPOINTMENTS AND ELECTIONS

The administrative bodies set up by the Statute for the Administration of the Provinces were made up of both appointed and elected officials. The highest posts, such as those of governor, were generally state appointments. The lower, elected posts were designed to encourage nobles, many of whom had made no contribution to local government since compulsory state service ended in 1762, to play their part once more. But the nobles did not respond as the empress had hoped. The posts to which they could be elected had little prestige and the pay was not high enough to tempt them. Local government was also rather dull, so many nobles preferred to join the army. In addition, there were not enough nobles in some areas to fill all the posts.

Many retired army officers became judges.

THE COURT SYSTEM

The complexity of the system of courts set up by the 1775 Statute, with different courts for each social estate, caused great confusion. If the plaintiff and the defendant were from different estates, it was hard to know where a trial should take place. The new equity courts never worked properly at all. Lack of legal training among the majority of officials was also a serious problem. Many judges were former military officers.

BRIBERY AND CORRUPTION

Bribery and corruption had always dogged Russia's legal system (*Source 6*). The rich were usually able to buy the verdict they wanted. Catherine's reforms did little to change this situation. Many officials of the old system moved to the new system, where they continued as before (*Source 7*). The courts' work was also hindered by a general lack of respect for justice among officials (*Source 8*). Drunkenness in court, laziness, and failure to keep proper records were all very common.

LIVING OUTSIDE THE LAW

Another drawback to Catherine's reforms was that they barely affected the serfs. Justice was usually administered to them either by their communes or their masters (*Source 9*). In addition, people in newly acquired regions of Russia, such as the former Polish lands, were not bound by Russian law, so the new courts were not able to enforce laws there.

THE ILLUSION OF PROGRESS

Catherine's administrative reforms resulted in more officials and rising costs (*Source 10*). However, the poor quality of the officials, the nobles' failure fully to participate, and the preservation of the serfs' position outside the system meant that little real progress was made.

Catherine kept her papers in this portfolio.

SOURCE 8

. . . in spite of the greater emphasis on legality fostered by Catherine, the attitude of Russian society and of the bureaucracy to law and justice remained largely unchanged in her lifetime. The very idea of legality, of a system of formal rules, valid yesterday, today, and tomorrow for everyone was quite alien to Russian society at all levels.
(EXTRACT FROM *RUSSIA IN THE AGE OF CATHERINE THE GREAT*, BY ISABEL DE MADARIAGA)

SOURCE 9

Communes in villages of all categories of peasants selected constables and watchmen. . . . When necessary, constables carried out preliminary investigations to find the perpetrators of crimes. Enforcing law and order merged into administering justice. For minor offences, constables arrested miscreants [wrong-doers] and punished them on the spot. For more serious crimes . . . communes had rudimentary courts and judicial procedures. . . . Only very serious crimes, such as murder, or disputes with members of other communes were referred to higher, official courts.
(EXTRACT FROM *THE RUSSIAN PEASANTRY 1600-1930*, BY DAVID MOON)

SOURCE 10

YEAR	ANNUAL COST OF LOCAL ADMINISTRATION (RUBLES)
1774	1,712,465
1785	5,618,957
1796	10,921,388

JUDGE
FOR YOURSELF

CATHERINE'S FOREIGN POLICY—A CAUSE FOR PRIDE OR SHAME?

Catherine the Great considered foreign policy central to her role as empress. Her achievements are clear—she won several wars and acquired large areas of land for her country—but they were accomplished at great cost to the Russian people, to the national finances, and to her own reputation. In fact, some experts now believe it was in her adventures abroad that Catherine served Russia least well. So should her foreign policy have caused her shame rather than pride? Read both sides of the argument and the sources, then judge for yourself.

A CAUSE FOR PRIDE?

SOURCE 1

3. All I hope, all that I wish is that this country in which God has cast me, should prosper . . . the glory of this country is my glory. . . .
36. To join the Caspian Sea with the Black Sea and link both of these with the North Sea . . . would mean elevating the Empire to a greatness far above other Asiatic and European Empires. What could resist the unlimited power of an autocratic prince ruling a bellicose [warlike] people?
(EXTRACT FROM CATHERINE'S PRIVATE PAPERS)

SOURCE 2

. . . and look the sleeping cat has woken up, and look it is going to chase the mice, and look you will see what you will see, and look everyone will be talking about us, and look none of them expected us to make all the commotion that we are making, and look the Turks will be defeated. . . .
(EXTRACT FROM A LETTER WRITTEN BY CATHERINE IN DECEMBER 1768, PREDICTING SUCCESS FOR THE REBUILT RUSSIAN NAVY)

EARLY YEARS

Even before she came to power, Catherine recorded her empire-building ambitions (*Source 1*). However, she spent the early part of her reign restoring Russia's finances after the Seven Years' War. In 1763, she also appointed a new foreign policy adviser, Nikita Panin.

WAR AGAINST THE TURKS

The first major foreign-policy challenge Catherine faced was war with the Ottoman Turks in 1768. She approached the conflict enthusiastically (*Source 2*), hoping to seize the Black Sea and end Muslim power in Europe. This was impossible, but her navy's victory at Chesmé (*Source 3*) and the later efforts of her armies eventually defeated the Turks. The 1774 Treaty of Kutchuk Kainardji that ended the war brought Catherine important territorial gains.

Catherine II in 1787, at the time of the Second Turkish War.

THE FIRST PARTITION

These acquisitions of land were not the first that the empress had made. During the war, in 1772, Russia, Prussia, and Austria each helped themselves to a large area of Poland's territory.

Called the First Partition, this action gained Catherine an additional 34,700 square miles (90,000 sq km) or more to rule over, as well as about 1,300,000 new subjects.

MEDIATING ROLE

The success of Catherine's troops in Turkey steadily enhanced Russia's reputation. By the 1770s, it was accepted as a major nation by more established powers such as Prussia and Austria. As a result, Russia was able to act as a mediator in the 1778–1779 War of the Bavarian Succession between Austria and Prussia. It also played a role during the American Revolution by organizing the League of Armed Neutrality.

Nikita Panin

MORE SUCCESS

Catherine's successes continued in 1783 with the annexation of the Crimea. The Second Turkish War, which began in 1787, was a far more substantial enterprise; it was the first major step in the Greek Project. When Grigory Potemkin, commander of Russian forces, began to collapse under the strain, it was the empress who urged him on (*Source 4*). The war ended in victory for Russia in 1791, and the Treaty of Jassy gave Russia still more land.

SWEDEN AND POLAND.

From 1788 to 1790, Russia also fought a war with Sweden. In the 1790 Treaty of Verela that brought this war to an end, Catherine stopped the Swedes from taking Russian land. Late in her reign, she also managed both to quash revolution in Poland and to gain even more territory (*Source 5*). The Second Partition of Poland, in 1793, and the Third, in 1795, brought her Lithuania, much of the western Ukraine, Courland, and more.

PRIDE AND POWER

Catherine the Great had good reason to be proud of her foreign-policy achievements. She strengthened Russia's position as a European power, led her forces to two major victories against the Turks, and greatly expanded both Russia's territory and the country's influence to the west and south.

SOURCE 3

My fleet, which was not under the command of my admirals but of Count Aleksei Orlov, first defeated the enemy fleet then burnt all its ships in the port of Chesmé. . . . Almost one hundred vessels of all types were reduced to ashes. I hardly dare to state the number of Muslims who perished: it could have been as many as 20,000.
(EXTRACT FROM A LETTER SENT BY CATHERINE TO VOLTAIRE ON SEPTEMBER 16, 1770)

SOURCE 4

Courage! Courage! I am writing this to my best friend, my child, my pupil, who sometimes shows more resolution than myself; but at the moment, I am braver than you because I am in good health and you are ill. . . . I feel that you are as impatient as a five-year-old child, when the work entrusted to you demands, at present, unshakeable patience.
(EXTRACT FROM A LETTER SENT BY CATHERINE TO POTEMKIN, 1787)

SOURCE 5

Now, a number of unworthy Poles . . . are trying to scatter and spread a pernicious new doctrine.
. . . For these reasons, Her Imperial Majesty is now pleased to take under her power all lands, towns, and regions enclosed within the new frontier line between Russia and Poland, so that [they] may stand under the sceptre of the Russian empire.
(EXTRACTS FROM CATHERINE'S *PUBLIC PRONOUNCEMENTS ON THE PARTITION OF POLAND*)

CATHERINE'S FOREIGN POLICY—A CAUSE FOR PRIDE OR SHAME?

A CAUSE FOR SHAME?

SOURCE 6

There was indeed in Catherine's whole attitude to the problem of the dissidents [Catholics] an insensitiveness which goes beyond mere diplomatic arrogance or clumsiness. She had been brought up by a devoutly Lutheran father, but religion sat lightly on her and she had accepted Orthodoxy with ease. She had no personal experience whatsoever of the Catholic Church or of a Catholic country. . . .
(EXTRACT FROM *RUSSIA IN THE AGE OF CATHERINE THE GREAT*, BY ISABEL DE MADARIAGA)

SOURCE 7

MONTH/YEAR	RECRUIT LEVY
Aug 1787	2 in 500 men
Sept 1787	3 in 500 men

Number of recruits raised in two months: 92,375

SOURCE 8

The Man who goes as a Soldier is considered as Dead to his family. . . . To be rejected is a great triumph. . . . Happy he who is lame, deaf, blind or maim'd, (& by the by they often cut off a joint of a finger or cut a limb as the time for recruiting approaches & that 'tis known who is to be chosen).
(EXTRACT FROM *THE RUSSIAN JOURNALS OF MARTHA AND CATHERINE WILMOT* 1803-1808)

EARLY YEARS

Catherine the Great's outward success in foreign policy concealed many flaws that gravely weakened the nation she ruled. They were apparent from early in her reign, and they grew more serious as the years passed.

CATHERINE AND POLAND

The 1768 uprising in Poland that led to the First Turkish War was partly due to Catherine's treatment of the country's Catholics (*Source 6*). The situation was made worse by her allowing Prussia too much influence.

Without the intervention of Frederick II, she might have compromised with the Polish government and avoided years of strife. As it was, brutality characterized Catherine's relationship with Poland ever after.

THE FIRST TURKISH WAR

The First Turkish War brought military glory for Russia. However, the war also diverted Catherine from the work of the Legislative Commission and was so costly that taxes had to be increased. From July 1769, the *obrok* demanded from state peasants went up to two rubles per person. Only serfs were exempt from the rise. High taxes and conscription fed the unrest that led to riots in Moscow during the 1771 outbreak of plague.

Alexander Suvorov, a Russian general.

THE FIRST PARTITION

The First Partition of Poland in 1772 marked a serious failure of Russian foreign policy. Frederick II of Prussia engineered the

Partition by warning Catherine of Austria's plans to join Turkey against her and telling Austria of Catherine's plans to keep the land she had won on its border. In this way, Frederick forced both Russia and Austria into accepting a scheme that was greatly to Prussia's benefit. Russia was left having to share power in a country where, before, it had had no real rivals.

THE GREEK PROJECT

In the 4th century A.D., Emperor Constantine I made the city of Constantinople a second Roman capital, and it became the heart of the Byzantine Empire. Centuries later, Catherine hoped her Greek Project would lead to the formation of a similar empire that another Constantine, her grandson, could run. The Second Turkish War was part of this unrealistic plan. Like the First Turkish War, it was a military success, but it led to great loss of life. In times of war, the recruit levy (the proportion of the male population that the government required to join the army) forced many more Russians than usual to become soldiers (*Sources* 7 and 8). Alexander Radishchev attacked Catherine for the death and misery she caused in this way (*Source 9*).

Emperor Constantine I

THE FATE OF POLAND

The last major foreign-policy events of Catherine's reign were the Second and Third Partitions of Poland. With these partitions, Russia, Austria, and Prussia wiped a proud nation from the map. At the same time, Catherine failed to help Austria, Prussia, and Britain hold back revolutionary France. Her only true concerns were the preservation of her own power and the settlement of conflicts on Russia's immediate borders.

A CAUSE FOR SHAME

Catherine the Great's foreign policy was no cause for pride (*Source 10*). Not only did it cost thousands of lives and a great deal of money, it also led to unrest at home and destroyed Poland. Furthermore, it never even brought the decisive victory over the Ottoman Turks for which the empress longed.

SOURCE 9

Thine is the blame if a mother lament for her son, or a wife for her husband, killed on the field of battle, for the danger of being subjects to a conqueror's yoke hardly justifies the murder called war. Thine the blame if the field be deserted, if the peasant's little ones starve at their mother's breast. . . .
The army was without discipline; my soldiers were valued less than cattle.
(EXTRACT FROM A DREAM SEQUENCE IN *A JOURNEY FROM ST. PETERSBURG TO MOSCOW*, BY ALEXANDER RADISHCHEV)

'The murder called war.' What do they want, to be left defenceless to fall captive to the Turks and Tatars, or to be conquered by the Swedes?
(CATHERINE THE GREAT'S RESPONSE TO THE ABOVE)

SOURCE 10

On the surface, judging by the size of her conquests, Catherine's foreign policy was extremely successful. Yet it is here, in the field in which she prided herself most on her skill, that she did the greatest disservice to Russia. Whereas in domestic policy her instinct was sure, and she knew how to conciliate opinion [bring people to an agreement], in foreign affairs she was both brash and brutal. . . . Catherine was fortunate that the victories of her armies covered up the flaws in her diplomacy.
(EXTRACT FROM *RUSSIA IN THE AGE OF CATHERINE THE GREAT*, BY ISABEL DE MADARIAGA)

WAS CATHERINE A MURDERER?

Soon after Catherine the Great came to power, two former czars died in suspicious circumstances. They were her husband, Peter III, and a 23-year-old who had ruled Russia briefly as Ivan VI. Did the empress play any part in these murders, both of which strengthened her position? Or was she an innocent leader caught up in the activities of others? Did she even know that the men's deaths were planned? Read the story and the sources, then judge for yourself.

SOURCE 1

I beg your Majesty to be truly sure of me and to have the goodness to remove the guards of the second chamber, because the chamber I am in is so small that hardly can I move, and, as she knows that I always walk about my room, it will make my legs swell up.
(EXTRACT FROM ONE OF PETER III'S LETTERS TO CATHERINE)

SOURCE 2

Little Mother, he is no more. But it never occurred to anyone, how could anyone think of raising a hand against our sovereign lord. But sovereign Lady, the mischief is done. He started struggling with Prince Fyodor at the table. We had not time to separate them and he is no more. I don't remember what we did but all of us are guilty and worthy of punishment. Have mercy upon me if only for my brother's sake. . . .
(EXTRACT FROM ALEKSEI ORLOV'S LETTER ANNOUNCING PETER III'S DEATH)

THE MOVE TO ROPSHA

After Catherine the Great seized power in the coup of June 1762, the deposed czar, Peter III, was confined in a country estate called Ropsha. The empress allowed him to take his dog, his violin, and his servant to this new residence, but sent his mistress to Moscow. The plan was, supposedly, to keep him there until he could be moved to the Schlüsselburg fortress, where Ivan VI was already languishing.

Guards swear allegiance to Catherine after the 1762 coup.

PETER IN PRISON

Peter did not cope with his new situation well. He cried a great deal and sent Catherine tragic letters asking her to improve his circumstances (*Source 1*). She did not reply, but hearing that Peter was ill, she allowed a doctor to be sent to him. Despite granting him some comforts and medical care, the empress must have realized that the former emperor would always be a threat. He had a stronger claim to the throne than she, and there were many Russians who supported his return.

THE ORLOV BROTHERS

Grigory Orlov, then Catherine's lover, and his brother Aleksei had masterminded the coup in which Catherine had seized the throne. Aleksei was placed in charge of the troops who were guarding Peter III at Ropsha. In early July, Catherine received a note from him explaining in a confused way that the former czar was dead (*Source 2*). Most historians think that Aleksei strangled or suffocated Peter in order to strengthen the empress's position and free her to marry Grigory.

DID CATHERINE KNOW?

Aleksei Orlov's letter makes no mention of carrying out Catherine's orders, but many people at the time were convinced of her involvement. The former czar's death certainly suited her, and she issued a manifesto that covered up the true facts of his passing (*Source 3*). In 1771, Aleksei told a French diplomat that "he felt very sad, being a humane person, to have had to do what was expected of him."

Grigory and Aleksei Orlov

IVAN VI

The circumstances surrounding Ivan VI's death were different. Since he had been deposed by the Empress Elizabeth in 1741, Ivan had spent his life in prison. On her accession, Catherine restated an old ruling that his guards were to kill him rather than let him escape. At the same time, she tried to persuade Ivan to become a monk, as monks were not allowed to become czars.

SUDDEN DEATH

Vassily Mirovich, an army lieutenant with a grudge against the empress, had other plans. He wanted to free Ivan VI and place him on the throne, in the hope that this action would bring him as much benefit as Catherine's coup had brought the Orlovs. Late on July 4, 1764, with other soldiers, he took over the Schlüsselburg fortress, and he read out a proclamation written allegedly by Ivan himself (*Source 4*). When Ivan's two guards heard the commotion, they stabbed the former czar to death, in accordance with their orders.

INNOCENT OR GUILTY?

Catherine, though horrified at the manner of Ivan's death, was also relieved that the young man was no longer a threat to her. After the murder, Mirovich, who had harmed no one, was beheaded. The guards who killed Ivan, by contrast, were promoted and given rewards. This outcome led many people to believe that the whole episode was a plot hatched by the empress to rid herself of a rival (*Source 5*). In truth, her only involvement in Ivan's murder was the giving of the order that he should be killed rather than be allowed to escape.

SOURCE 3

On the seventh day of our accession to the throne of Russia, we have been advised that the ex-Tsar Peter III suffered another of his habitual haemorrhoidal attacks, together with a violent colic. Aware of our duty as a Christian, we immediately gave the order to supply him with all necessary care. But to our great sadness we received, last night, the news that God's will had put an end to his life.
(EXTRACT FROM CATHERINE'S MANIFESTO OF JULY 7, 1762)

SOURCE 4

Not long had Peter III possessed the throne when by the intrigues of his wife and by her hands he was given poison to drink, and by these means and by force the vain and spendthrift Catherine seized my hereditary throne.
(EXTRACT FROM THE MANIFESTO READ ALOUD BY MIROVICH)

SOURCE 5

The moment and circumstances of this murder have made people suspect the Empress of having instigated it herself with the object of removing a source of continual worry to her.

The people believe that this performance took place only to decently get rid of Ivan.
(EXTRACTS FROM REPORTS OF TWO FOREIGN AMBASSADORS TO THE RUSSIAN COURT)

GLOSSARY

anti-Semitism: prejudice against and persecution of Jews.

assigned peasant: a state peasant sent to carry out industrial work (for example, in a factory or mine), who is still legally attached to the state rather than having becoming the property of the industry owner.

autocracy: government by a single ruler with unlimited authority.

bail: the temporary release of a defendant from custody in exchange for a deposit of money. The money is not returned to the person who pays it if the defendant fails to appear in court at the appointed time.

Balkans: a peninsula in southeastern Europe that was largely controlled by the Ottoman Empire during Catherine the Great's time. The Balkans now contain Romania, Bulgaria, Greece, Albania, the states that once made up Yugoslavia, and the European part of Turkey.

barshchina: compulsory labor done by serfs as a form of payment to their masters.

boyar: a member of the highest aristocratic rank in Russia during the 16th and 17th centuries. The rank was abolished by Czar Peter the Great in 1722.

Byzantine Empire: a Christian empire of western Asia and eastern Europe that grew up around the ancient Greek city of Byzantium. In the 4th century A.D., the Roman emperor Constantine I made Byzantium the eastern capital of the Roman Empire, giving it the new name of Constantinople. After Rome, the western capital of the empire, fell in the 5th century A.D., the Byzantine Empire developed separately. It was eventually overrun by the Ottoman Turks in 1453.

chamberlain: the official in charge of managing a noble or royal household.

chin (plural chiny): any of the fourteen ranks in the Table of Ranks issued by Czar Peter the Great in 1722.

civil court: a court that hears cases relating to an individual's rights and duties as a private citizen. Civil courts deal with cases regarding property or contracts, not cases relating to crimes such as theft or murder.

commune: a unit into which both serfs and state peasants were organized to ease the process of government, law enforcement, land distribution, and tax collection.

Cossack: a warrior horseman or peasant belonging to one of several separate communities (for example the Don Cossacks) in southeastern Russia. The Cossacks came increasingly under state control during the 1700s.

court peasant: a peasant who worked and lived on land owned by Russia's imperial court.

craft guild: in Western Europe, an organization of craftspeople that acted to regulate their craft, for example, by controlling apprenticeships. Czar Peter the Great intended the Russian craft guilds he set up in 1721 to do the same, but they never became powerful enough.

czar: the title used by Russia's emperors. It is a form of the Roman title "Caesar."

despot: a ruler with absolute power, especially one who misuses that power; a tyrant.

duma: any of the town councils established by the 1785 Charter to the Towns.

Enlightenment: an 18th-century philosophical movement that emphasized the importance of reason and science. The Enlightenment also encouraged reforms, including educational reforms, based on these new ideals.

enserfment: the turning of free people into serfs.

estate: a major social grouping within imperial Russian society. Under Catherine, there were four estates: serfs, state peasants and Cossacks, nobles, and townspeople.

Freemason: a member of a secret, all-male organization first established in the Middle Ages by a group of stone-workers (masons). The modern organization was founded in 1717 and has members in many professions. Freemasons believe in God and do charitable works, but they have often been accused of unfairly favoring their fellow members in business deals.

French Revolution: the rebellion against the French monarchy that broke out in 1789, which resulted in the proclamation of a republic in 1792 and the execution of King Louis XVI in 1793.

garrison: a military base, normally containing accommodations for troops and surrounded by a defensive wall or fence.

General Procurator: a high-ranking official of Russia's central government in St. Petersburg whose role was to supervise the operation of courts and local government bodies throughout the country.

Greek Project: Catherine the Great's plan to reestablish the Byzantine Empire and place her grandson, Constantine, as its emperor.

Gregorian calendar: the calendar introduced by Pope Gregory XIII in 1582 and still in force today. The old Julian calendar was used in Britain and its colonies until 1752, and in Russia until 1918.

guberniya **(plural** *gubernii***):** any of the major territorial divisions in imperial Russia; known in English as provinces.

Holy Roman Empire: an empire that covered the German states, Austria, and several other European countries, lasting from 800 to 1806. Its rulers saw themselves as successors of the Roman emperors.

house of correction: a prison to which people were sent for committing a variety of offenses, from disobedience to nonpayment of taxes.

Huguenot: A French Protestant who believed the strict teachings of 16th-century Christian theologian John Calvin.

Julian calendar: the 365-day calendar introduced by Roman statesman Julius Caesar in 46 B.C. that differed from the Gregorian calendar mainly by having more leap years.

Kremlin: the walled central area in Moscow containing Russia's imperial palaces, cathedrals, and other important buildings.

land lease: a legal agreement granting a person the right to use a piece of land for a fixed period of time, usually in return for payment.

Lutheranism: the form of Protestant Christianity based on doctrines formulated by the 16th-century German theologian Martin Luther.

manifesto: a public declaration of plans and policies made by an individual ruler or government.

*obrok***:** money, goods, or both that serfs and other peasants gave to their masters in return for use of the masters' land.

Ottoman Turks: members of a Turkish people whose first ruler was the 13th-century sultan Osman. From his reign onwards, the Ottoman Turks expanded their territory, eventually overrunning the Byzantine Empire in 1453. The Ottoman Empire reached its height in the 16th century, and it came to an end only in 1918, after World War I.

poll tax: a tax that every adult was required to pay and that did not vary according to income or wealth.

principality: a territory governed by a prince.

protectorate: a territory controlled by, but not formally annexed to, another state.

republic: a state with an elected government and no hereditary ruler, such as a king or emperor.

Romanov dynasty: the imperial family that ruled Russia from 1613 to 1917.

ruble: the Russian unit of currency.

Russian Orthodox Church: Russia's national branch of the Eastern Orthodox Church. Eastern Orthodox Christianity is characterized by elaborate ritual, and it is practiced in many countries other than Russia, including Greece.

Russian Revolution: the rebellion against imperial rule that broke out in Russia in 1917, resulting in the establishment of a Communist government under Vladimir Lenin and the execution of Czar Nicholas II and his family in 1918.

Senate: the main central government institution of imperial Russia. In her 1763 reform of the Senate, Catherine the Great divided it into six departments and restricted its law-making powers.

serf: beginning in 1649, a privately owned Russian peasant with very few personal rights.

Seven Years' War: the war between Austria, France, and Russia, on one side, and Britain and Prussia, on the other, that lasted from 1756 to 1763. The war took place mainly in Europe, but the French and British also fought in North America, where both had colonies.

state peasant: a Russian peasant who lived and worked on state-owned land. State peasants had far more rights than serfs.

Synod: the governing body of the Russian Orthodox Church, established by Czar Peter the Great in 1721.

uezd **(plural** *uezdy***):** any of the local government districts into which *gubernii* were divided.

*ukaz***:** a decree made by an emperor.

*Ulozhenie***:** the Russian legal code established in 1649, during the reign of Czar Aleksei Mikhailovich Romanov.

War of the Austrian Succession: the war fought mainly between Austria and Prussia over who should succeed the Holy Roman Emperor Charles VI in 1740. Russia sided with Austria, but a peace treaty was signed in 1748, before Russian troops were called on to fight.

War of the Bavarian Succession: the war that broke out between Austria and Prussia in July 1778 over Austria's attempt to acquire parts of Bavaria, a German state. Mediation between the two sides by Russia and France led to the signing of a peace treaty in May 1779.

workhouse: an institution that provided basic food and shelter for the healthy, noncriminal poor.

INDEX